BILL GATES
SPEAKS

Insight

from the

World's Greatest

Entrepreneur

~ ❋ ~

BILL GATES SPEAKS

Insight

from the

World's Greatest

Entrepreneur

BY JANET LOWE

John Wiley & Sons, Inc.

New York • Chichester • Weinheim • Brisbane • Singapore • Toronto

Copyright ©1998 by Janet Lowe. All rights reserved.

Published by John Wiley and Sons, Inc.
Published simultaneously in Canada

This publication is designed to provide accurate and authoritative
information in regard to the subject matter covered. It is sold with the
understanding that the publisher is not engaged in rendering professional
services. If professional advice or other expert assistance is required,
the services of a competent professional person should be sought.

Library of Congress Cataloging-in-Publication Data
Lowe, Janet
   Bill Gates speaks: insight from the world's greatest entrepreneur /
   Janet Lowe.
      p.   cm.
   Includes bibliographical references.
   ISBN 0-471-29353-9 (cloth: alk. paper)
      1. Gates, Bill, 1955–   . 2. Microsoft Corporation—History.
3. Businessmen—United States—Biography. 4. Computer software
industry—United States—History. I. Lowe, Janet. II. Title.
HD9696.63.U62G374   1998
338.7'610053'092—dc21
[b]   98-25931

Book design and composition by Anne Scatto / PIXEL PRESS

~ • ~

This book is dedicated to Austin,
with a prayer for
lasting peace in Ireland.

~ • ~

CONTENTS

PREFACE

William Henry Gates III, cofounder and chairman of Microsoft Corporation, has been astonishingly successful at many things.

* His pioneering work in personal computer software has altered all our lives. In 1997 virtually all businesses and fully 40 percent of American homes had computers. Soon 66 percent of all homes will be furnished with the square little monitors with blinking cursors. More than 80 percent of those personal computers will light up with flying windows on the screen, the signature of Microsoft's Windows operating system. Gates "is to software what Edison was to the light bulb—part innovator, part entrepreneur, part salesman, and full-time genius."[1]

* Gates obliterated the incorrect yet persistent notion that big ideas come only from philosophers, writers, or academic circles. As *Forbes*

publisher Rich Karlgaard explained, "The old distinction between ideas and products, between ephemera and ingots, is evaporating."[2]

* Gates is more than a mere corporate executive. A cultural icon, he is the godhead, the sun king, the very soul of Microsoft, the company that made him a billionaire by age 31, and before he was 40, the wealthiest American ever.

* Gates is a survivor, in fact the victor, in a savage industry with little history, few traditions, almost no manners, and certainly few established methods of operation. Some of those deficiencies are being resolved in courts around the world at this very moment.

And, by chance, Gates excelled at something else. He brought to a roiling boil all the conflicted feelings our society has about capitalism—our national longing for economic success and dominance, and our anger, anxiety, and fear of abuse when someone actually achieves it.

To understand how strongly some people feel about Gates, log onto the Internet and check out the Web sites created simply to flame him, some of which seriously debate whether Gates is actually the devil in disguise.

From the Bill Gates Joke Page: "What do you do if you're trapped in an elevator with Timothy McVeigh,

Saddam Hussein, and Bill Gates, and you have only two bullets in a gun? Shoot Bill twice just to make sure."[3]

An invective against Gates is not confined to the Internet. Mitch Kapor, inventor of Lotus 1-2-3 and former head of that company, called Gates "brilliant, powerful, highly successful, ruthless, and an unethical person. I think anybody who plays with a 'win at all cost' strategy and cuts off the oxygen of the competition is unethical. And he is the dominant and most successful example of that."[4]

ComputerWorld magazine describes Gates's situation:

> . . . Just a few years earlier, he had been celebrated as the scrappy entrepreneur who courageously carved a thriving business from the technological wilderness ignored by entrenched powers. Now he was a maligned bully who wanted to own the entire software universe, a greedy man who thumbed his nose at both customers and competitors.
>
> Which was the real Bill Gates? The richest American by virtue of his roughly 22 percent stake in Microsoft, Gates was an object of envy and awe, paranoia and adulation. These strong emotions made a balanced assessment of his actions impossible.[5]

Gates often is compared to flamboyant leaders of the industrial revolution. The correlations have some validity. Those men profited in some way from technological advances that forced changes in the way people lived, says Nathan Myhrvold, Microsoft's resident futurist and imagineer of new technology. Myhrvold explained that between 1875 and 1900, new inventions, including the typewriter, the telephone, internal combustion engine, and the zipper, sprang up everywhere.

> And the popular press glorified a new aristocracy of wealth and ingenuity; people like Thomas Edison and Alexander Graham Bell, Andrew Carnegie and John D. Rockefeller. In retrospect, it seems inevitable that a few strong-minded individuals would see opportunities and rush to capitalize on them; betting on the industrial age was not a task for faceless committees. Their gambles made them vastly rich and gave them and their extravagant possessions enormous celebrity.[6]

But it isn't just his wealth and celebrity status that makes Gates so fascinating.

He is puzzling in that his accomplishments and his demeanor don't match. His crackly, high-pitched voice, his slang (super cool, neat, totally random, high bandwidth), hair that seems to be at odds with his scalp, and his trademark Mr. Rogers sweaters do not seem to befit a mogul. The dissonance was extremely noticeable in the early Gates, who started his business at 19 but still looked like an adolescent at 30.

To steal his own terminology, Gates is a "rich" target for cartoonists and comedians. When anyone in the computer industry crisscrosses his arms and rocks back and forth like an autistic child, everyone knows the person is mimicking Bill Gates. Although Gates has filled out in recent years and obviously makes regular visits to the barber, the image of a skinny, unkempt wunderkind just won't go away. Gates's early mop of dandruffy hair prompted Scott McNealy, chief executive of Sun Microsystems to dub Microsoft Windows a "hairball" that just keeps growing.[7]

Vanity Fair magazine called Gates a 13-year-old trapped in a robber baron's body. An "unlikely captain of industry, his calm, monotone style of delivering a speech hides his energy and intensity."[8]

Gates's image problem partly stems from the fact that he stepped into the public eye at an amazingly young age. The stories of his first years in business reveal a bratboy-genius. He was notoriously acerbic, condescending, even rude. As we've watched an overcharged but gifted kid grow up, it's been like watching the youthful Mozart. Not necessarily a pretty sight, but the product leaves us breathless.

Even as he reaches middle age, Gates remains difficult to quantify. His tales of Microsoft's mercurial rise sometimes seem a shade overblown, but his business analysis and vision of the future are right on the bulls'-eye. He has cautiously made his way into marriage, parenthood, and philanthropy with the media dogging every step. When Microsoft came under scrutiny by state and federal governments for its business practices, Gates realized he should cultivate a warmer, friendlier, and more tolerant public image. Reviews of his transformation so far indicate that he still needs practice.

His personal growth aside, Gates's greatest challenge now is helping Microsoft grow gracefully and profitably old. Longevity is rare in the field of high technology, and even old-timers like IBM have had a bumpy ride. Yet Rockefeller, Edison, Bell, and the early industrialists to whom Gates is compared, created companies that prospered and survived for another century. Their businesses became bedrocks of the economy. Although constantly scrutinized and sometimes disassembled by the antitrust regulators or by poor management, descendants of the original corporations remain industry leaders today. Gates has turned his attention to ensuring that Microsoft will join their ranks. And because he started so young, he has ample time to devote to the task.

∼

Now, some guidance on reading *Bill Gates Speaks*. This is not a book about technology, though technology is there. It is not a blow-by-blow account of how Microsoft became a global business leader in less than 20 years, though readers will learn about that too. This book was not written to expose Bill Gates as the Great Satan or the Great Savior. Readers must decide that for themselves.

It *is* a book that acknowledges the impact Gates has had on the world in terms of technology, economics, and social direction. It is about a precocious "technoid" who plays a leading role in changing the way we work, play, heal, study, and go about daily life. It's a book about *what* and *how* Bill Gates thinks and what we can learn from him.

My apologies if I have used too many acronyms or abbreviations, or too much jargon. A section called "E-Cabulary" (electronic vocabulary) has been included to help those who need translations.

The book is not presented in chronological order but rather by subject matter. Please refer to the time line at the back or to the notes for dates and places the remarks were made.

The editorial staff of John Wiley & Sons, Inc., Myles Thompson and Jennifer Pincott in particular, have been wonderfully supportive of this project, and I wish to thank them. Thanks also to Austin Lynas, Alice Fried Martell, Karen Johnson, Brenda Stevens, Jolene Crowley, and countless others who were so generous with their time and ideas.

Although this is not a book about computers, I bow to the computer books tradition. *Bill Gates Speaks* was written on an AT&T NEC PC with an Intel Pentium chip running Windows 95 and WordPerfect 8. But trust me, Windows 95 had no influence on the content except to make sure the book got done.

~

No matter how Gates is portrayed in history, there is no question that he is the premier business celebrity of our time. A Nexis database search in 1997 showed that Gates was mentioned 8,433 times that year by the mainstream media. A *Fortune* magazine poll showed that 73 percent of company executives considered Microsoft one of America's great businesses.

At *Inc.* magazine's conference of 500 leading entrepreneurs in September 1997, the group overwhelmingly chose Gates as their "most admired" entrepreneur. Gates took 59 percent of the vote; media mogul Ted Turner, 8 percent; Apple Computer's Steve Jobs, 5 percent; information age millionaire Ross Perot, 4 percent; and Waste Management Inc. founder Wayne Huizenga, 3 percent.[9]

A Merrill Lynch survey of corporate information officers done about the same time, however, showed that 59 percent believed that Microsoft abused its power. On the other hand, the same poll showed that 62 percent believe that the U.S. Justice Department should give in and allow Microsoft to integrate its Internet Web browser and operating system.[10]

Although Gates has not yet helped us reach consensus on how capitalism should be waged, he has helped focus our attention on the issue. In the meantime, the battle to comprehend Bill Gates goes on. "Love him or hate him, but you can't ignore him," wrote *Fortune* managing editor John Huey.[11]

GROWING UP GATES

YOUNG JUMP

A fresh-scrubbed, blue-eyed, towheaded little boy with a cowlick that grew very much like his mother's, smiles out from Bill Gates's childhood pictures. The photos belie the fact that Gates was a superactive kid, always up to something. He repeatedly crammed himself into a box, then leaped out, measuring how much farther he could jump each time. In his teens and even later, he would suddenly spring up to touch tree limbs, door jambs, or anything overhead that caught his eye.

Those spontaneous bursts of energy inspired a Japanese cartoonist to name the character he modeled after Gates, Young Jump. Like Gates, the popular Young Jump is relentless in his pursuit of high-tech adventure.

Gates was a middle child and only son, with a sister one year older and another sister nine years younger. He was nicknamed "Trey" by his Grandmother because of the "III" following his name. Trey is a cardplayer's term for three. Descended from early settlers of Washington state, the family was close-knit and financially secure. Bill Sr., and Mary Maxwell Gates met and married while still in college. Gates's father was a partner in a prominent Seattle law firm, his mother, a former teacher, was unusually well-connected and active in Seattle's social and civic life.

~

As a baby, Gates was happiest when rocking away on his rocking horse; as an adult, Gates still rocks when he is concentrating or is under stress. He was easily bored.

> *"As a student I took notes with either hand, using my right hand when I was bored and wanted a small challenge."[1]*

In the sixth grade, Gates was underperforming in school, at war with his mother, and generally struggling with life. His parents decided to send him to a psychologist for counseling.

Gates thought the counselor was "a really cool guy. He gave me books to read after each session, Freud stuff, and I really got into psychology theory."

After working with the boy for a year, the counselor presented Gates's mother with some disturbing news. It was useless to force Bill to conform to traditional behavior or to be more obedient:

"You're going to lose. You had better just adjust to it because there's no use trying to beat him."[2]

~

Gates took trombone lessons for a while, pored over Edgar Rice Burroughs's Tarzan and Martian stories. When he was seven years old, Gates decided to read the entire encyclopedia. He got to the Ps before moving on to a new hobby. He devoured biographies of famous men, such as Franklin D. Roosevelt and Napoleon, learning everything he could about the French emperor.

> *"When I was a kid science was very interesting because all those moon shots were going off. We could learn about liquid oxygen and escape velocity. Now most of the space program has become so commonplace that it doesn't inspire a thirst for knowledge the way it once did."³*

~

The Gates family attended the University Congregational Church, where the Reverend Dale Turner was pastor. Each year Turner promised to buy dinner at Seattle's 606-foot-tall Space Needle restaurant for all those in the confirmation class who memorized the Sermon on the Mount. Although 31 others stuttered and stammered their way through chapters 5, 6, and 7 of the Book of Matthew, Turner was astounded when Bill learned the passages on a family car trip to the coast and then delivered a flawless recitation.

"I needed only to go to his home that day to know that he was something special. I couldn't imagine how an 11-year-old boy could have a mind like that. And my subsequent questioning of him revealed a deep understanding of the passage," Turner said.[4]

Turner conceded that Gates probably didn't learn the verses for their spiritual value, but because he loved a challenge.

> *"Growing up, my parents always encouraged us to read a lot and think for ourselves. They included us in discussions on everything from books to politics. In the summer, we'd go up to Hood Canal where our family and several other families who gathered there every year would play a lot of competitive games—relay races, egg tosses, Capture the Flag. It was always a great time, and it gave all of us a sense that we could compete and succeed."[5]*

Gates says his memory is not photographic but merely very good, especially for material that deeply engages him.

> *"I can still remember all my lines in a high school play,* Black Comedy. *I was so afraid that I'd forget the lines that I just burned them into my head."[6]*

He became the master of the business deal early. Gates negotiated a contract with his older sister, Kristi, to use her baseball glove whenever he wanted to, on a nonexclusive basis. For that right he paid $5 and required her to sign a contract.

Gates rose to the rank of Eagle Scout, a life member of Troop 184. On one mountain hike, Gates's new boots gave him such painful blisters that his mother had to drive to camp and take him home. Nonetheless, Gates credits scouting for giving him "an environment that encouraged learning and curiosity."[7]

~

To cover up his difficulties in public school, Gates often played the class clown. That changed when his parents decided he should have an education more specifically suited to his needs. Gates was enrolled in Seattle's exclusive and rigorous Lakeside School.

> *"Then I went to private school, and there was no position called the clown. I applied for it, but either they didn't like my brand of humor or humor wasn't in that season. In fact, I didn't have clear positioning for a couple of years. I was trying the no-effort-makes-a-cool-guy routine. When I did start trying, people said, 'Oh, we thought he was stupid! Better reassess.'"[8]*

~

Gates spent the summer of 1972 as a congressional page. Already an experienced businessboy, Gates continued his entrepreneurial ways that summer when he and a friend bought 5,000 George S. McGovern–Thomas Eagleton presidential campaign buttons for 5 cents each after Eagleton was dumped from the ticket. The buttons quickly became collectors' items. Gates and his friend resold the buttons for many times what they paid for them, sometimes as much as $25 each.

⁓

Ed Roberts, founder of MITS, the company where Gates and Allen first got their start, claims that Gates achieved success so early that he didn't fully work his way through his youth.

"He's kind of like Elvis Presley," Roberts says of Gates. "He never got to grow up."[9]

⁓

Yet age has tempered Gates in some ways:

> *"I don't jump spontaneously the way I used to, in the early years of the company . . . or even in a meeting . . . Now the jumping is not that common."[10]*

Maybe not, except when challenged to a dare by his soon-to-be wife:

At a Microsoft party, Gates was dared to jump over a table. It was a formal affair, and Gates was wearing a tuxedo and slippery, patent-leather shoes, which made the leap more treacherous. But he hopped right over the table. Melinda French then placed a lighted candle on the table and dared him to try again. When he jumped that, she kept adding more candles. Gates took longer and longer running starts, as the gathered crowd laughed and cheered him on.[11]

The Gateses have a massive trampoline in their new Lake Washington estate.

IS BILL GATES BORDERLINE AUTISTIC?

There is speculation that Bill Gates is borderline autistic, a question that may never be fully answered. Autism is a mysterious, much studied but little understood behavioral condition, although it is known that autistic children often are born into families where both parents are highly intelligent. *Time* magazine once compared Gates's traits to those linked with autism:

- Excellent ability in highly targeted, logical, abstract thinking

- Sudden panics, rages, or other uncontrollable emotional outbursts

- Reluctance to make eye contact

- Tendency toward repetitive or automatic movements, such as spasm, tics, or rocking

- Fondness for trampolines or jumping.[12]

LAKESIDE MOTHER'S CLUB

Parents who doubt they can have a positive influence on their own children's education should remember the Lakeside School Mother's Club. In 1967 the mothers used proceeds from a rummage sale to install a crude computer terminal (actually, an ASR-33 Teletype machine that for an hourly fee, connected to a

General Electric Mark II computer elsewhere) so students could experiment with this newfangled gadget.

Gates's father said that his seventh-grade son soon became hooked—"Completely engrossed."[13] Soon Gates and his pals ditched classes to hang out at the computer center; by eighth grade, Gates was earning spending money as a programmer.

Nearly a dozen Lakeside students became pioneers in the computer software field, Bill Gates and Paul Allen—cofounders of Microsoft Corp.—foremost among them.

~

Gates seemed deliberately to get bad grades in the subjects that didn't interest him, yet he has been autodidactic, or self-taught, in many subjects since he was a child. At age 13, he taught himself computer programming.

> *"The notion was that, of course, the teachers would figure out this computer thing and then teach it to the students. But that didn't happen. It was the other way around. There was a group of students who kind of went nuts."*[14]

~

> *"To look back now and think—geez, how did I get addicted to something like that? It's hard to understand. They didn't get a special phone line. We shared a phone line with the business office. So we were always competing to try to get on the thing and staying in late at night. The janitors were always kicking*

us out. It wasn't a computer. We had to dial out to the
computer. Computers were so expensive that you could
only time-share the computer. The GE computer we
were connected to cost $4 million."[15]

~

Gates may be a technology whiz, but after a visit to
Seattle, Jay Leno joked:

"He's not necessarily so different from the rest of
us. I went into his den last night and his VCR is still
flashing 12:00."[16]

THE COMPUTER ROOM GANG

Lamont Benson, a neighbor of Paul Allen's, recalls:

"I remember always seeing the lights on in Paul's
room at 3 a.m. He would be up there with that Gates
kid, working on computer stuff."[17]

~

Although Gates was not disciplined about housekeep-
ing, personal hygiene, or driving habits, he liked the
tidiness of writing computer programs:

"Running your program is the absolute test. You write
a program, try it, and it either works or it doesn't."[18]

~

Gates was thrown out of the student's club, the Lakeside Programmers, because he was two years younger
than Allen and the others, and they thought he was
too immature. When the club couldn't do without him

they invited him back, but Gates set the terms. He was in charge of the projects after that.

~

Lakeside math teacher Fred Wright recalls that Gates had a talent that applied well to programming: "Bill had the ability to see shortcuts."[19]

~

When the computer room gang ran up large hourly charges with the time they spent on the Mother's Club computer, the device had to go. Soon, however, a mother came up with an incredible opportunity. In the late 1960s, Gates and members of the Lakeside Programmers rode bicycles, took the bus, or bummed rides each afternoon to the Computer Center Corporation (C-Cubed) office, where, in turn for free time on a new Digital Equipment Corporation computer, they searched for programming errors.

Each evening at 6:00 P.M. C-Cubed employees filed out of their offices as the three high school students arrived. "We stayed up until all hours of the night because we just loved working on software so much. It was a fun time," recalls Allen.[20]

Gates and his buddies produced a 300-page manual called *The Problem Report Book*, which was used by C-Cubed's professional programmers.

Gates said he and his friends never wrote computer viruses, which he explained were unknown at the time because computers were not networked together. While

he can't understand the pleasure of destroying someone's work, Gates does understand why people enjoy
the challenge of outsmarting a computer system.

> *"When I was a teenager, getting a computer to crash
> was a big deal. It was a way to learn."[21]*

~

> *"We were fortunate to be authorized to 'hack' the
> system, but back then even unauthorized hacking
> caused minimal problems."[22]*

~

The kids took the opportunity to learn machine language surreptitiously.

> *"Paul would hoist me up on the garbage cans and
> I'd get the [programmer's] notes out with the coffee
> grounds on them and study the operating system."[23]*

~

Gates's lust for pushing the limits finally got him in
trouble when he broke into a protected program. The
user's password told the computer which areas each
user was entitled to enter and which was off limits.
Just for fun, Gates wiggled around the password protection, which gave him access to the host company's
financial and other information. The little adventure
caused the operating system to crash, and Gates's for-
ays into confidential information were discovered. His
parents ordered him to take a leave of absence from
computers, which he did.

"I swore off computers for about a year and a half—the end of the ninth grade and all of the tenth. I tried to be normal, the best I could."[24]

⌇

Before long, Gates was back, and the computer club was taking on jobs to pay the costs for computer access. The members started a business using a computer to count cars driving along designated streets. Traf-O-Data earned $20,000 before its clients went looking for more sophisticated service providers. Some observers dispute the Traf-O-Data's profitability, and most of the records, including the program itself, have been lost. Gates and Allen say, however, that the little company was a test run in the business world and that they learned a lot. By then Gates says:

"... I was a hard-core technoid."[25]

⌇

Like all teenagers, Gates and his friends looked for ways to seize power from their teachers:

"The greatest scam we discovered was that by getting the job doing high school scheduling, we could decide exactly what boys and girls were in our classes, and that was an incredible reward. It really motivated us to learn how to write interesting software."[26]

During the summer Gates and Allen earned approximately $5,000 in computer time by programming class schedules.

~

One night an office furniture rental company came into C-Cubed and took the chairs out from under the boys while they were working. Gates and his friends got a firsthand lesson in what "bankrupt" meant.

Gates and Allen were frustrated at their difficulties in finding another computer. They finally bought their own 8008 chip so that the two, along with friend Paul Gilbert, could build their own. Gates came up with $360, and when the chip arrived all wrapped up in aluminum foil, it seemed so magical that the boys were almost afraid to touch it. Their work building a computer convinced Gates and Allen that they should stick to the software business.

Nevertheless:

> *"When we were teenagers, Paul Allen taught me a lot about computer hardware and encouraged me to believe in—and bet on—the microprocessor. I was lucky enough, at a young age, to discover something that I loved and that fascinated me—and still fascinates me. And I was lucky to have parents who motivated and encouraged me."*[27]

~

Gates says that until Paul Allen started teaching him about computers and computer chips, he considered becoming a lawyer or a scientist:

> *"I couldn't decide which. My dad was a lawyer, but scientists seemed to have more interesting jobs than lawyers did."*[28]

Even so, Gates did not see a clear career path in computing. It "was not a mainstream thing. I didn't see myself as a hacker forever."[29]

PRACTICING ON THE POWER GRID

Playing games and fiddling around on computers was never enough. Early on Gates and Allen dreamed of owning a software business:

> *"In fact we had been very frustrated because we'd been calling up people like IBM and Digital and saying, 'Would you like our compiler or would you like our editor?' and they said 'No, we do that stuff ourselves and you guys are just high school kids anyway. Why do you keep calling us up with these things?'"[30]*

~

Their chance to do serious programming came when engineers working on the Northwest power grid ran into trouble and, in searching for answers, discovered the C-Cubed *Problem Report Book*. TRW Inc. was in charge of writing programs to analyze the electricity needs of the Columbia Basin, then control the amount of electricity the dams generated. But bugs in the PDP-10 computer program were slowing them down. *The Problem Report Book* identified a huge number of the bugs, plus the names of two programmers who discovered them—Bill Gates and Paul Allen. TRW tracked the programmers down and asked them to come to Portland, Oregon, for job interviews.

"No one knew we were just in the ninth and tenth grades."[31]

~

They were hired anyway. Gates took a work-study leave from Lakeside and went to Portland, where he and Allen got an apartment, then reported to work for programmer John Norton. Norton dazzled the young hot shots with his ability to memorize the operating system's 5,000-page listing. Norton, says Gates, challenged him to do better work.

"I have an image in my head of this person named Norton that I met at TRW. He always showed me when I wasn't doing super well. So if I'm sloppy or lazy, I always imagine that he's going to walk up, look at the program, and tell me, 'Look, here's a better way to do that.'"[32]

Gates returned home and graduated from high school in 1973, after scoring a perfect 800 on the math portion of the Scholastic Aptitude Test.

~

Vernon Harrington of Lakeside School, wrote a letter of recommendation to Harvard on Gates's behalf. In part, it read:

"As a tenth grader Bill Gates was famous as Lakeside's ranking computer freak. The boy genius who was quicker at mathematical computations than his teachers and who with two friends contracted to set up a payroll tape for a Portland firm. The job was com-

15

pleted. They were paid off in $5,000 worth of computer time—time which they later used in computerizing the school's schedule."[33]

Harrington added that in his last two years of high school, Gates branched out, taking an interest in politics and drama while at the same time continuing to read omnivorously.

HEADING OFF ON THE CONVENTIONAL ROAD

HARVARD

Bill Gates won admission to Princeton, Yale, and Harvard as a National Merit Scholar. He chose Harvard and entered in the fall of 1973. Gates was a typical freshman in many ways, thrown off pace by the new requirements and a higher level of competition. He skipped classes, spent days on end in the computer lab working on his own projects, played poker all night, and slept in a bed without sheets when he did go to bed. Other students recall that he often went without sleep for 18 to 36 hours.

~

Even at Harvard, Gates followed his old pattern of getting good grades in subjects he liked and disdaining those that were of little interest. His heart didn't seem to be in his studies. Gates joined few college activities unless his friend Steve Ballmer dragged him off to a party.

Gates and Ballmer, an applied math major, became lifelong friends and eventually Ballmer joined Gates at Microsoft:

"He [Ballmer] was the opposite of me. I didn't go to classes much, wasn't involved in campus activities. Steve was involved in everything, knew everyone. Steve was general manager of the football team, head of the lit[erary] magazine, ad manager of the Crimson [newspaper]. He got me to join the Fox Club, a men's club where you put on tuxedos, smoke cigars, drink too much, stand up on chairs and tell stories, play pool. Very old school."[1]

~

Part of his problem was that Gates couldn't decide what he *really* wanted to do with his life:

" . . . everything seemed so attractive, and when you had to pick a specific one you had to say no to all the others. I'd think, well, if I went to that law firm some partner might not like me, and they might assign me to these crummy cases, and I'd think well, God, *that could really be* crummy.*'"[2]*

~

As a result, Gates spent a lot of time brooding:

" . . . sitting in my room being a philosophical depressed guy, trying to figure out what I was doing with my life."[3]

~

Although he wasn't the brightest math student at Harvard, Gates started taking graduate-level math as a freshman and generally got As.

THE PANCAKE PUZZLE

"The chef in our place is sloppy, and when he prepares a stack of pancakes they come out all different sizes. Therefore, when I deliver them to a customer, on the way to the table I rearrange them (so that the smallest winds up on top, and so on, down to the largest at the bottom) by grabbing several from the top and flipping them over, repeating this (varying the number I flip) as many times as necessary. If there are "n" pancakes, what is the maximum number of flips (as a function of "n") that I will ever have to use to rearrange them?"

Harvard Computer Science Professor Christos Papadimitriou says the seemingly simple problem had proved very stubborn. Bill Gates, however, considered the puzzle similar to the challenges faced in writing a complex computer program. His solution was long but ingenious. Professor Papadimitriou wrote up Gates's explanation, and in 1979 it was published in the *Journal of Discrete Mathematics*. The breakthrough Gates made on the math problem has remained on the cutting edge. The professor later gave the puzzle to other students, vowing that if they solved it, he would go to work for them, as he should have done with Gates.

Gates and Ballmer took a graduate economic theory course together. They were the only undergraduates in the course but attended few classes.

> " . . . we fell so far behind that, during what was called 'reading period,' we had to work all night to try and figure out what the heck was going on and we kept thinking that we had a big advantage because we were math students. We understood math and these poor economic guys, they didn't really understand math at all. So we thought we must have a big advantage, but whenever we took the practice quizzes, we weren't doing too well. We just worked and worked and really—Steve and I—that was a key part of getting to be close friends."[4]

Professor Michael Spence says both Gates and Ballmer got an A in the class.

∽

Despite his up-and-down experience at Harvard, Gates says:

> "It concerns me to hear young people say they don't want to go to college because I didn't graduate.
> "For one thing, I got a pretty good education even though I didn't stay long enough to get my degree. For another, the world is getting more competitive, specialized and complex each year, making a college education as critical today as a high school education was at one time."[5]

∽

Furthermore, says Gates:

"I loved my years at college and, in many respects, I regretted leaving. I did it only because I had an idea—founding the first microcomputer software company—that couldn't wait."[6]

~

When Harvard bored him, Gates applied for computer-related jobs in the Boston area. Digital Equipment was one of his favorite places to interview because they picked applicants up at the Boston airport in a helicopter and flew them to corporate headquarters. Gates encouraged Paul Allen to try for a job as a programmer at Honeywell so the two could continue work on their dreams for a software company. Allen and his girlfriend jumped in his old Chrysler New Yorker and drove out to Boston. Soon Gates's life took a dramatic change of course.

LEAVING HARVARD TO CHASE A DREAM

Paul Allen made an exciting discovery one frigid December day as he crossed Harvard Yard after visiting Gates. The January, 1975 issue of *Popular Mechanics* was on the newsstand, and on the cover was a picture of the revolutionary new microcomputer kit, the MITS Altair 8080.

Allen bought the magazine and raced back to persuade Gates that they should develop a language for the simple little machine.

~

The Altair 8080 had 256 bytes of memory (compared to 8 million or more in most personal computers today) but no software.

"Paul kept saying, 'Let's start a company. Let's do it.'"[7]

～

"We realized that the revolution might happen without us. After we saw that article, there was no question of where our life would focus."[8]

～

Gates and Allen called Ed Roberts, founder of MITS, and promised an Altair program before they had written it.

"We were getting about 10 letters a day from people. I would tell them, 'Whoever writes it first gets the job,'" said Roberts.[9]

The two friends rushed to a Harvard computer to write an adaptation of the BASIC language program.

～

The MITS Altair 8080 was not the original micro-computer, but it was the first to catch the imagination of the public. Inexpensively priced, it attracted hundreds of orders from electronics enthusiasts.

Gordon Moore, one of the founders of Intel and author of the famous "Moore's Law" (See "Thinking About Someday"), recalled that there wasn't much to the Altair:

"You know the first MITS—I guess you'd call it a PC now—the Altair; it was just a hobby device where the inputs were toggle switches and the outputs were LEDs.

You could demonstrate the way a computer worked, but it was a tough way to do any practical computing."[10]

~

According to Gates, the Altair was just a box with blinking lights:

"It was actually kind of a kit for $360, and you had to put it together. And even once you did that, it really didn't do much for you, but just the challenge of making it work and sort of trying to figure out what it could and couldn't do made it very popular."[11]

~

"MITS didn't understand the importance of it. Nobody did. But we knew that people in schools everywhere would have these computers."[12]

~

Gates and Allen believed computers could perform wonders:

"And so our slogan from the very beginning was 'a computer on every desk and in every home.'"[13]

~

Allen and Gates's passion to work on the first readily available personal computer turned out to be justified:

" . . . the PC is the mainstream, the mainstream of all computing. It's fair to say that it's become really the tool of the information age."[14]

BACK ON THE HIGH-TECH HIGHWAY

"THE COOLEST PROGRAM I EVER WROTE"

After Gates and Allen promised software to Roberts, Gates expropriated the mainframe computer at the Aiken Computer Center at Harvard, which was meant for student projects, not for commercial work. Since they didn't have an Altair 8080 computer, Gates and Allen had to figure out how it functioned from the magazine article and simulate it on the big Harvard computer.

> *"We just had this book that described the machine. If we had read the book wrong, or the book was wrong, we were hosed."[1]*

The two young men worked through February and March 1975 in Gates's dormitory room, madly writing code.

> *"It wasn't a question of whether I could write the program, but rather a question of whether I could squeeze it into 4K and make it super fast."[2]*

Gates's gift for simplicity did the trick.

"It was the coolest program I ever wrote."[3]

～

Allen flew off to Albuquerque to demonstrate the raw software to Roberts. At the last moment, Allen realized they'd forgotten to program a start prompt. He hurriedly added it, then held his breath as he loaded the program onto the Altair. It worked.

～

When Allen returned to Harvard triumphant, the friends celebrated by going out for sodas and ice cream. The 19-year-old Gates ordered a Shirley Temple.

～

Gates and Allen sold their BASIC language to MITS for $3,000 plus royalties.

～

Allen says that when he arrived in New Mexico to further develop the program that would become the industry standard for the next six years, he had to beg a loan from Roberts to rent a motel room. He'd spent all his money on his airplane ticket. But Roberts was impressed with the young man, and soon Allen was on the payroll as MITS software director. In June 1975 Gates took a leave of absence from Harvard to join Allen. Although he returned the following fall, his heart and mind were back in Albuquerque. He took a second leave and never returned to college.

"My parents weren't all that excited about their son announcing he was dropping out of a fine university to start a business in something almost nobody had heard of called 'microcomputers.' But they were always very supportive."[4]

~

The BASIC program is forever etched in Gates's memory:

"I can visualize the source code to the version of BASIC that I wrote for the first microcomputer, back in 1975. That was the programming code that got Microsoft started, so maybe it's no surprise that I can still see every detail of the first page, the second page, the third page—as if they were in front of me."[5]

~

Gates once said BASIC for the 8080 was his favorite among the software programs that he has written, " . . . because of the effect it's had, and because of how appropriate it was at the time, and because we managed to keep it so small."[6]

~

Gates says BASIC probably will continue to be the first language used by student programmers because it is easy to learn and because ingenious uses have been found for it. It was the first language that Gates and his teenage pals in Seattle learned in the late 1960s.

"I have a soft spot in my heart for BASIC. It was Microsoft's first product, written in my college dorm room."[7]

NOTE: There are many languages in BASIC, or Beginner's All-purpose Symbolic Instruction Code; Gates's version simply became the first standard for microcomputers.

～

"Sometimes I envy people who still get to program. After I stopped programming for Microsoft, I used to say half-jokingly in meetings: 'Maybe I'll come in this weekend and write it myself.' I don't say that anymore, but I think about it."[8]

ON-THE-JOB TRAINING

Before leaving for Albuquerque, Allen and Gates kicked around company names—Outcorporated Inc., Unlimited Ltd., Allen & Gates came to mind. Micro-soft seemed the obvious choice. Once they were settled in New Mexico, Gates and Allen recruited former members of the Lakeside Programming Group (and other pals), and Micro-soft was on its way. About the time they moved the company to the Seattle area the hyphen was dropped and the name became Microsoft.

～

Though the Gates-Allen partnership started out a 50/50 deal, Gates later bargained for a 60/40 split in his favor. Gates felt it was fair, since in addition to their subcontracting work, Allen was drawing a salary from MITS. As a Microsoft employee, Gates worked only for royalties. Gradually, over the years, Gates has sold shares until now he owns about 22 percent of the company.

In the early years Microsoft's management style was loose. Both Allen and Gates did a bit of everything. Generally, however, Allen pushed new technology and products, while Gates focused on new business, negotiations, and contracts. Within 18 months the two had earned a few hundred thousand dollars for their new company by writing programs for Apple Computer Inc. and Commodore.

One of the aggravations of being a junior entrepreneur was that Gates couldn't rent a car because he wasn't 21. When he visited Applied Digital Data Systems, a terminal manufacturer in Hauppauge, New York, Gates had to ask his clients to pick him up at the airport.

~

Allen, Gates, and their reconstructed computer room gang continued to live and work unconventionally. First they stayed at the dusty Tumbleweed Motel, then they later cut costs by sharing apartments. Most of their time was spent programming, eating pizza, and dashing out for a movie or to streak through the desert at midnight in Gates's Porsche.

"Yeah, life for us was working and maybe going to a movie and then working some more. Sometimes customers would come in, and we were so tired we'd fall asleep in front of them."[9]

~

About a week after Miriam Lubow was hired as office manager, she noticed a kid entering Gates's office. Gates had been out of town, so she rushed off to tell co-worker Steve Wood that someone had gone into the room that nobody was allowed to enter without permission. She was astounded to learn that the kid was her boss. Perhaps as a subtle way to warn customers of the owners' youthfulness, Microsoft advertisements in electronics magazines featured a cartoon character, the small but mighty Micro Kid.

~

Microsoft soon was involved in its first of a long string of lawsuits, both by and against the company. The computer industry, it turned out, lives by litigation.

NOTE: One industry newsletter claimed that Intel sued companies that tried to bring to market a chip that competed with the highly successful Intel 386 chip. Even if Intel often lost the suits, they slowed the competition and crippled competitors with legal bills.

~

Microsoft's contract with Roberts called for MITS to make "best efforts" to sell Microsoft BASIC rather than Microsoft selling software directly to customers.

But soon there were so many illegal copies of the language floating around that MITS no longer tried to sell the program. Gates was irate because he felt

MITS's attitude only encouraged piracy. (See "Battling Pirates.")

Gates consulted his father, who assured Bill that he could win if he sued to retrieve the rights to BASIC. Bill Sr. helped his son find an attorney in Albuquerque. By then Roberts had sold MITS to a company called Pertec.

Gates and Allen agreed to let the suit against Pertec go to arbitration because they thought it would be quicker than a trial and likely appeals. But arbitration moved at a snail's pace, and Pertec withheld payments until a decision was reached. Microsoft nearly went broke:

> *"They were trying to starve us to death. We couldn't even pay our lawyer. They tried to get us to settle, and we almost did, it was that bad. The arbitrator took nine months to issue his damn opinion. But when it was all over, the arbitrator ripped them apart for what they had done."*[10]

~

The mediator was especially harsh on Pertec and Ed Roberts because they had not respected the initial agreement with Microsoft. He called it the "ultimate case of business piracy."[11]

~

Ed Roberts insisted that his company financed the development of the BASIC software and was its legitimate owner but admits he should have paid more attention to the contract:

"I was naive," Roberts said. "It sounds self-serving now, but I was really concerned with not trying to screw those guys. Bill was only 19 and Allen only a couple of years older, but it turns out they were a lot older than I was—Bill for sure. Paul is a totally honorable guy."[12]

⁓

Although Gates may have been able to borrow money from his parents, he did not. Microsoft was bootstrapped from the beginning. Since then Gates has always kept large cash reserves so that Microsoft can weather future crises.

⁓

In 1979 H. Ross Perot, chairman of the computer service company EDS, tried to buy Apple Computer and, when that failed, approached Microsoft. Perot thought that Bill wanted too much money for the company—he recalls Gates asking for $40 to $60 million, although Gates says he wanted between $6 and $15 million. Perot says he later kicked himself for not clinching the deal. By 1998 Microsoft employed 25,000 people in 58 countries. By then a large number of current and former Microsoft employees were millionaires, and three had become billionaires.

⁓

After Microsoft's falling out with Pertec, there was no reason to stay in Albuquerque, where few customers were willing to visit. Business was on a solid footing, and Gates and Allen were ready to move on. By the time the company relocated to the Seattle suburb of Bellevue, Microsoft had a solid corporate culture.

"Bill Gates is Microsoft," said Alan Brew, a San Francisco branding consultant. "The character of the whole company is cloned in the form of this combative, young, arrogant leader."[13]

～

In addition to Gates and Allen, the original Microsoft employees were Steve Wood, Bob Wallace, Jim Lane, Bob O'Rear, Bob Greenburg, Marc McDonald, Gordon Letwin, Andrea Lewis, and Marla Wood. When, in 1979, one of the group got a coupon for a free photo, they gathered for a group shot just days before moving to Bellevue. The computer-fixated change agents looked like they'd just piled out of a Volkswagen van on arrival at a rock concert.

～

Gates was notorious for his fast and reckless driving, and he was in a particular hurry to get home to Seattle. On the way he got three speeding tickets.

MICROSOFT'S GROWING PAINS

"The software business is very American. The original technological advances were all made here. The largest markets are here. And the atmosphere that

allowed it all to happen is here. That's how our original customers, including IBM, could be so open-minded about buying from a 25-year-old guy with a small company out in Washington. They may have thought it was crazy at the time, but they said, 'Hey, if he knows so much about software, maybe he knows even more.'"[14]

~

Gates was 25 years old and Microsoft had only 32 employees—when it was approached in 1980 by the undisputed king of the computer industry, IBM.

Gates didn't look old enough to vote, "Yet here was a young man wise well beyond his years—a genius at programming and a born master of his business, gifted with remarkable instincts when it came to controlling what would be his company's extremely profitable relationship with IBM," said an IBM executive.[15]

When IBM telephoned for an appointment, they asked to see Gates the very next day. He quickly rescheduled a meeting with Fred Kassar, chairman of the computer game company Atari. The decision, plus a few others that followed, would make Gates a billionaire by age 31.

~

On their first visit to Microsoft, IBM executives arrived at the door and asked an unkempt young man the way to Bill Gates's office. The youngster accompanied the executives back to the office, then sat down behind the desk. The men did not realize until then that they'd met Microsoft's chairman.

On their next visit, IBM executives dressed in casual slacks and cotton knit shirts, only to discover that Gates had dressed up, donning a three-piece suit and tie for the occasion. The meeting started off with a good laugh.

～

IBM, the Rolls-Royce of computer companies, called the moves with subcontractors. Nevertheless, it had fallen behind in the personal computer industry and sought outside help with its next foray into the rapidly expanding small computer market. IBM executives in Boca Raton, Florida, hoped to explore the idea with Microsoft of devising an operating system for an IBM computer for individual use. Microsoft had not yet produced its own operating system, so Gates referred IBM to Microsoft's frequent partner, Digital Research. When IBM's talks with Digital Research went nowhere, IBM returned to Microsoft.

～

After a meeting of the national board of United Way, Mary Gates approached board member John Opel, chairman of IBM. She commented that his company had started to do some work with her son Bill and that she was sure they would like working with him. Opel did not acknowledge the remark. Later, when developers of the personal computer were presenting their plans for the yet-unborn machine to IBM's

Management Committee, Microsoft's name came up. Opel asked, "That wouldn't be Mary Gates's boy Bill, would it?" From then on Gates was considered to have connections at IBM.[16]

~

In what must be the deal of the century, Gates paid a Seattle Computer Products programmer, Tim Patterson, $50,000 for a rudimentary operating system he'd written called 86-DOS, or Q-DOS, for Quick and Dirty Operating System. Gates modified Patterson's work, named it MS-DOS (Microsoft Disk Operating System), and sold it to IBM. For the sake of speed, IBM decided to build the PC as an open platform, meaning that it could be replicated easily. Lucky break. The new machine would become the universally popular IBM PC. Microsoft delivered the operating system—the soon to be ubiquitous MS-DOS—in 1981. Soon some 100 other companies obtained MS-DOS licenses so they could build similar machines that would be IBM compatible. Overnight MS-DOS became the industry standard.

Other major PC manufacturers, including Sony, Matsushita, and NEC, also turned to Microsoft for their operating systems, and sales at Microsoft skyrocketed.

~

Microsoft made the final transition from a start-up to a professionally managed company in 1980 when Gates hired his former Harvard classmate, Steve Ballmer, as personal assistant to the president. Gates was vacationing in the Caribbean on a sailboat called the *Doo-Wah, Doo-Wah* when he negotiated Ballmer's job conditions.

> " . . . *I was going off on this vacation and I have to negotiate the salary with Steve. So we were on this ship-to-shore radio phone, where I kept saying, 'Doo-Wah, Doo-Wah! Over!' I think we started at $40,000. Everybody else on my vacation had been drinking and they kept saying, 'Pay him whatever it takes! Get somebody to help you out! You look like you're really stressed out!' So I agreed to pay $50,000. Which of course, turns out to be like 10 to the minus fifth portion of [Ballmer's] compensation . . .*"[17]

In addition to his salary, Ballmer was given stock in the company, which by 1997 was worth some $7 billion.

~

Microsoft has grown up with the software industry. The Business Software Alliance reported that the U.S. software industry added $67 billion to the economy in 1996, ranking behind only the motor vehicles and equipment industry ($106 billion) and the electronic components and accessories' industry ($78 billion).

HAVE A HARD-CORE WORK ETHIC

Microsoft is infamous for working its employees hard—but few work harder than Bill Gates himself.

Between 1978 and 1984 Gates took only 15 days off work, including four days he squandered at a tennis ranch near Phoenix.

The cafeteria at Microsoft headquarters in Redmond is open until midnight to allow for people who work late. "Anything with caffeine is free," joked one employee. Actually, all beverages in the Microsoft cafeteria are free.[18]

"If you don't like to work hard and be intense and do your best, this is not the place to work."[19]

~

A major dispute arose between IBM and Microsoft while they worked together programming OS/2, IBM's replacement for MS-DOS. IBM claimed its people wrote a lot more code (programmed more lines) than Microsoft did, and therefore Microsoft workers were slacking. Microsoft programmers insisted that the number of lines programmed was meaningless. The idea was to get the code written as concisely as possible. Writing less was good, but it took more time.

"Microsoft is designed to write great software. We are not designed to be good at other things. We only know how to hire, how to manage, and how to globalize software products. The key was to never view ourselves as a service company."[20]

~

Brad Silverberg, a senior vice president who guided the development of Windows 95, Internet Explorer, and other Microsoft products, went off on a bicycle ride across the United States in the summer of 1997 and by June 1998 still hadn't returned to work on a full-time basis. The 43-year-old Silverberg said he hadn't broken ties with the company but was spending his time with his family as well as running, hiking, and snowboarding.

This sort of situation often arises, reported *The Wall Street Journal*, when employees work very hard for long periods of time and at the same time amass enough salary and stock that they no longer need to work. Microsoft has now formally established a sabbatical program for veteran employees.

> *"Like any company whose chief product is intellectual property, we face a challenge finding and keeping the very best people. Universities and other progressive companies have long understood that one way to attract and keep the best people is to offer sabbaticals periodically so people who are working very hard can take some time off to catch their breath, travel, get involved in community activities or whatever."[21]*

~

Microsoft isn't the only hard-core company in the computer industry: According to *Inside Intel*, Intel chairman Andy Grove yelled at his secretary for leaving work an hour early on Christmas Eve and subsequently circulated the so-called Scrooge memo to all employees ordering them in the future to work a full day on December 24.[22]

~

"How does Microsoft keep up such a [work] pace?" asked *MNC* editor Simon Walch in an America Online article. "One big reason: Bill Gates never sleeps. He's constantly looking for new revenue sources, even when his existing products are generating fat rivers of cash."[23]

~

But working hard isn't the only thing:

> *"Maintaining focus is a key to success. You should understand your circle of competence, the thing that you're good at, and spend your time and energy there."*[24]

~

> *"Today, I work because it's fun. In that sense, I guess you could say that I approach business as a kind of problem-solving challenge. That doesn't mean I don't take business seriously, because I do. But life's a lot more fun if you treat its challenges in creative ways."*[25]

GO PUBLIC FOR THE RIGHT REASONS

Although Microsoft did not need additional capital, in 1981 Gates and Allen sold 6.2 percent of the company to Technology Venture Investors, of Menlo Park, California, the Silicon Valley venture capital firm that would help convert Microsoft to a publicly-owned company.

~

Gates hesitated to take Microsoft public because he feared it would be distracting:

"The whole process looked like a pain, and an ongoing pain once you're public. People get confused because the stock price doesn't reflect your financial performance. And to have a stock trader call up the chief executive and ask him questions is uneconomic— the ball bearings shouldn't be asking the driver about the grease."[26]

~

Gates was compelled to make the move, however, so he could offer employee stock options and so all employees, including himself, could convert their assets to cash if necessary or desirable.

"We're using ownership as one of the things that ties us all together."[27]

~

Microsoft made an initial stock offering on March 13, 1986, at $21 per share. Within days the price rose to $35.50. When it hit $90.75, Gates became the youngest billionaire ever.

~

In January 1998 Microsoft stock split for the seventh time since going public. At that time, adjusted for splits, $10,000 invested in the initial public offering would have been worth $2.4 million.

"When we went public back in 1986, I owned about 45 percent of the total shares of Microsoft. That position has gradually declined during the past 12 years to something in the range of 22 percent currently. I sell Microsoft shares regularly to diversify my portfolio of investments, pay taxes, and so forth. Additionally, Microsoft has issued new shares over the years for acquisitions and to fund our employee stock option plans, so the total number of outstanding shares has increased. If I had never sold any shares of Microsoft stock, my holdings today would represent about 33 percent of the total. I intend to keep a sizable stake in the company because I am deeply committed to the future of this company and the exciting opportunities we have to deliver innovative products and solutions to our customers."[28]

Gates still doesn't like the distractions of being a public company. At board meetings he says:

"There is a lot of talk about how to stack the bricks of gold, rather than why is there still gold coming out of this machine."[29]

THE GATESIAN MANAGEMENT STYLE

THE PROPELLER HEADS

Call them propeller, digit, or gear heads, wonks, brainiacs, or Microserfs—Gates prides himself on hiring the smartest people he can find. It is the depth of talent at Microsoft, he said in 1992, that sets it apart from other companies.

> *"Take our 20 best people away and I tell you that Microsoft would become an unimportant company."*[1]

NOTE: Considering Microsoft's growth, that number may be larger now.

The bright minds are challenged at almost every step:

> *"Smart people ought to be able to figure things out, if they get enough facts."*[2]

"I'm not an educator, but I'm a learner. And one of the things I like best about my job is that I'm surrounded by other people who love to learn."³

⌒

Nathan Myhrvold, Microsoft's top creative thinker, says, "Bill is not threatened by smart people, only stupid ones."⁴

⌒

Although Microsoft's founders have reached middle age, Gates still likes to hire younger workers. The average age of a Microsoft employee is 34.3.

"Young people are more willing to learn, come up with new ideas."⁵

⌒

Former Microserf Rob Glaser, at age 31, cashed in his $15 million in Microsoft stock to start his own business. He is typical of other Microsoft propeller heads, explained one magazine writer:

"Like Microsoft, [he] was smart, young, perhaps a little hard to take, and convinced he was absolutely right about a lot of stuff. But that was what was rewarded at the company and everything was going too fast there for a lot of management training."⁶

⌒

How do you get do be a propeller head?

One way is to read *The Art of Programming* by Donald Knuth. There are three volumes, with more to come.

"If somebody is so brash that they think they know everything, Knuth will help them understand that the world is deep and complicated. It took incredible discipline, and several months, for me to read it. I studied 20 pages, put it away for a week, and came back for another 20 pages."[7]

Gates says anyone who can read the entire body of work should send him a résumé.

～

Journalist Randall Stross was skeptical of stories he'd heard about the company's brain power when he first began researching a book on Microsoft. But after three months of access to the company, Stross wrote:

"What struck me about Microsoft as I examined its operations at close range was not the company's market share but the intense, pragmatic thoughtfulness that informed its decisions. I observed no scolding 'THINK!' signs on the walls as in the IBM of yore, but 'THINK' permeated Microsoft's bloodstream through and through. This was a company of smart people, managed well, constantly learning as it went."[8]

～

Despite its good reputation, Microsoft is described by several former employees as "not friendly to women." Microsoft officials disagree.

Gates says that Microsoft has been lucky to hire a lot of talented people right out of college, and many have been women. The highest percentage of women at Microsoft work in marketing and project management; only about 20 percent of the people who actually write computer code are female. That's higher than the percentage of women in the computer schools from which Microsoft recruits, but it is still below Microsoft's goals.

"On the bright side, it is a much more balanced industry today than it was 15 years ago. Back then, it was a bunch of guys staying up all night."[9]

~

Gates has produced an estimated 1,200 Microsoft employee millionaires, with some estimates closer to 3,000. If you're not considered a propeller head, you may not become wealthy working at Microsoft. In fact, you may work there without having a real job.

The company has been fighting a lawsuit involving one of the paramount social issues at the dawn of the millennium—what constitutes a true employee and what defines a casual laborer. The decision also will have an impact on laws nationwide governing retirement benefits, hiring regulations, and other workplace policy.

Technical writers, receptionists, and other members of the Microsoft support team are increasingly "temporary" workers. They are contracted by outside employers who don't always offer health insurance, vacation pay, or the highly desirable Microsoft stock options.

According to the *Los Angeles Times*, approximately 27 percent of Microsoft's employees are temporary workers. In Silicon Valley, 40 percent of all workers are temps.

Eight disgruntled (and in some cases long-term) Microsoft temps filed a class action suit against the company, claiming they were thinly disguised employees and deserved employee status.

The policy dispute goes back many years. In 1990 the IRS decided that Microsoft's freelancers should be classified as regular employees under tax rules. Microsoft then discharged most of the temps, offering to rehire them through an outside staffing agency. Microsoft continues to interview and hire the workers, but the temporary employment agencies issue checks, withhold taxes, and the like. Up to 30 percent of workers' paychecks are withheld to cover the costs of these services. The temporary employment issue is particularly sensitive nationwide because many temp workers are women or are mature workers who aren't old enough to retire but need health and other benefits.

The case has been working its way through the court system, and in 1997 the U.S. Ninth Circuit Court ordered Microsoft to grant employee stock purchase plans and 401k benefits to contractors who were hired and supervised by Microsoft managers at company facilities and who met other benchmarks for "common-law" employees.

The temps are well paid by Washington state standards. A technical writer earns $25 to $35 per hour. However, excluding Microsoft's five best-paid executives, an average Microsoft employee earns about $220,000 per year counting salary and stock options.[10]

Temporary workers allow Microsoft to respond quickly to changes in market needs. Furthermore, says Steve Ballmer, Microsoft president, "A temp is a temp. Some people prefer to work as temps. People know when they sign up. It's not like we fool anybody."[11]

∼

Microsoft receives something like 10,000 unsolicited résumés a month. Some of the applications are duplicates, however, from people who apply in more than one division.

ASSEMBLE A BRAIN TRUST

The propeller heads are led by higher ranking Microsofties, members of the brain trust. Gates says:

> *"These are all supersmart guys who've grown up with the business. This team is an amazing group. None of these people are trying to push, or care that much about their title, or even how they are perceived externally."[12]*

At least a dozen top executives have been with Microsoft for many years, but the most visible of the group are the company's cofounder (and now a director) Paul Allen, current heir apparent to Gates's job Steve Ballmer, and chief of new technology Nathan Myhrvold. Japanese entrepreneur Kay Nishi once was a member of the brain trust but had a fallout with Gates several years ago.

~

Paul Allen left a full-time position at Microsoft in 1983 after being diagnosed with Hodgkin's disease. From the very beginning Allen was credited with counterbalancing Gates's wild intellect and energy with technical savvy and long-term vision.

Gates said of Allen: "I'm more aggressive and crazily competitive . . . running the business day to day, while Paul keeps us out front in research and development."[13]

Allen's illness has been in remission for more than 15 years, and he uses his estimated $15 billion to invest in high-tech and sports enterprises. He still owns about 9 percent of Microsoft, but also owns the Portland Trailblazer's basketball team and the Seattle Seahawks football team. He has a $500 million, 18 percent stake in Steven Spielberg's multi-media studio, DreamWorks SKG. Allen was an early investor in America Online and TicketMaster, though he sold his portion of TicketMaster to Barry Diller, chairman of the Home Shopping Channel. In all, Allen has positions in about 35 different companies.[14]

For fun, Allen developed the Experience Music Project, a museum in Seattle to honor Jimi Hendrix and other Pacific Northwest musicians. The $60 million, 130,000 square-foot museum displays a 6,000-piece collection of guitars, gold records, and other Hendrix memorabilia. In his spare time, Allen cranks up his Stratocaster to jam with his rock band, The Threads.

He has an estate on Seattle's Lake Washington and a villa in romantic Cap Ferrat on the French Riviera, and donates money to the SETI (Search for Extra-Terrestrial Intelligence) Institute.

Gates and Allen, according to some reports, have had a prickly relationship from time to time, but Gates says: "We still see this stuff the same way, and we debate about it and share ideas quite a bit. The thing that's totally amazing is that looking at the next 20 years, we both believe there's actually more opportunity to have a broad impact than in the past 20 years."[15]

∽

Time magazine once described Bill Gates as the King Arthur of the cyberelite. Steve Ballmer and Nathan Myhrvold represented the two poles of Gates's personality: Ballmer "a smooth-talking, savvy Lancelot; Myhrvold a techno-Merlin."[16]

∽

Ballmer and Gates have been pals since Harvard, when both attended a double bill of *A Clockwork Orange* and *Singin' in the Rain*. *Clockwork*'s violent antihero crooned the title song from the latter movie while bashing heads together.

Ballmer is not technical in the code-writing sense, but he was an undergraduate math major and is a supercharged business wizard. Gates regards Ballmer, who bangs on walls and shouts to make a point, as one of his closest friends and advisors. *Forbes* calls Ballmer Gates's "alter ego" and his "butt-kicking enforcer."[17]

> *"No one should doubt that he's number two in the company. Steve is my best friend."*[18]

~

The *New Yorker* printed this description of Nathan Myhrvold: "Myhrvold has the fair, smooth skin and a small nose of a child. His light-brown beard, large spectacles and dark suit give him the air of a kid dressed up for Halloween."[19]

Amusing, yes, but it is wrong to underestimate Myhrvold. He grew up in Santa Monica, graduated from high school at 14, from the University of California at Los Angeles at 19, earned his doctorate in theoretical physics from Princeton, and studied with British theoretical physicist Stephen Hawking at Cambridge. He once tried Formula One auto racing for fun, enjoys gourmet cooking, and drives a Humvee. One of his original ideas? Tapping a computer into the human spinal cord, although he admits there might be a major interface problem.

Gates bought Myhrvold's company in the early 1980s and eventually promoted him to chief technology officer to help build one of the all-time great research and development organizations. *Fortune* anticipates that this R&D dynasty will rank with the legendary Bell Laboratories, IBM's Thomas J. Watson

Laboratory, and Xerox's Palo Alto Research Center (PARC). Under a plan launched in 1991, Microsoft expects to have approximately 650 scientists working in labs around the globe (currently there are 280 in place).[20]

Why would Gates pour money into research that may not pay off for years, if ever?

"The only way to get access to strategic technology," said Myhrvold, "is to do it yourself."[21]

Gates says of Myhrvold: "He's a lot like I am. The same thinking he brings to a technology problem, he applies to business strategy."[22]

NOTE: For more, see "Bill Labs."

~

Kuzuhiko (Kay) Nishi once was considered Japan's own Bill Gates. The two met when each was just 22 years old. Nishi was publishing a popular Japanese hackers' magazine, *ASCII*, and distributing software. Like Gates, Nishi walked away from a prestigious university to become a cyberentrepreneur. Nishi heard of Gates, then called information in the United States to get his telephone number. When the operator asked which city, Nishi only knew Microsoft was based in New Mexico, so he tried Albuquerque. He found Gates and arranged to meet him at an upcoming computer conference. When Gates launched into the Japanese market in 1977, Nishi became his partner and for several years they were soul mates. The chubby, flamboyant Nishi built Japan into Microsoft's second largest market after the United States.

Nishi was extravagantly nutty and rude at times but also quite brilliant. He met Kazuo Inamori, president of Kyocera Corporation, on an airplane flight and convinced Inamori to invest in microtechnology. With Kyocera's support, Gates and Nishi developed one of the first portable microcomputers ever—the Radio Shack Model 100.[23]

Soon the high-living Nishi began piling up debts in Microsoft's name and once paged Gates at the San Jose airport to ask for a loan to pay for $275,000 of stock he'd purchased on a whim.

Gates arranged for Microsoft to bail Nishi out, reluctantly.

> *"Because Kay was Kay. What did I want, my best guy ever to go to jail for bad debts?"[24]*

The cheerful Nishi explained to *The Wall Street Journal*, "I am famous for random activities. I have many moods, high and low, and the difference is very big."[25]

Nishi and Gates parted ways in 1986 when Gates felt that Nishi had lost control. Since then Nishi has spoken harshly of Gates. Gates has been equally candid about his opinion of Nishi:

> *"The guy's life is a mess. He's worth negative half a million and I'm worth X million—that's certainly seeds for bitterness."[26]*

~

EMBRACE NERDISM

Gates looked pretty nerdy in puberty, but as he matures, fills out, and pays better attention to personal grooming, his appearance has improved. And aside from an adolescent-sounding voice coming from an adult head, he's never entirely conformed to the nerd image. He is athletic; is a skilled water skier, ice skater, card shark; and is fairly sociable. Gates enjoys dancing and music. Although he could easily become obsessed with a project in his early years, he has always had a wide range of interests. And as for the voice, it's become such a trademark that his audiences would be disappointed if he suddenly spoke in a deep, rich, baritone. What fun would that be to listen to?

～

To some, however, Gates still is the nerdiest. He made the cartoon pages—Bloom County paired the comic Bill the Nerd with Bill the Cat. Cartoonist Berkeley Breathed committed visual savagery on Gates, portraying him with a huge head and skinny neck. Breathed says he once saw Gates in line buying a movie theater ticket:

"He looked like he probably needed help buying that ticket; he doesn't fit; he's the kid that we made fun of in school."[27]

NOTE: Gates says that false sightings of him are common.[28]

～

Despite the stinging criticism, Gates doesn't think he's a nerd:

> *"If being a nerd means you're somebody who can enjoy exploring a computer for hours and hours late into the night, then the description fits me, and I don't think there's anything pejorative about it. But here's the real test: I've never used a pocket protector, so I can't really be a nerd, can I?"[29]*

~

Nathan Myhrvold goes one step better. He says nerdism has become cool. "Nerds like us can do lunch with anyone these days."[30]

PRACTICE DARWINIAN MANAGEMENT

Microsoft's management style has been described as Darwinian—survival of the fittest.

> *" . . . one of the lessons from the Darwinian world is that the excellence of an organism's nervous system helps determine its ability to sense change and quickly respond, thereby surviving or even thriving."[31]*

~

Like Darwin's theory of evolution, Microsoft's management mode can be brutal. According to G. Pascal Zachary, who wrote a book about the making of Windows NT, Gates uses a management style that is neither American (individualist) or Japanese (consensus driven) but uniquely its own. Zachary calls the style "armed truce." He writes: "Conflict is at the heart of every significant Microsoft decision. This is a company constantly at war, not only with outsiders, but also with itself."[32]

~

Microsoft's success depends on dedicated workers who have enormous faith in a charismatic leader, claims Scott Winkler, an analyst at Gartner Group:

"Bill tells them to do something and they do it. They believe in him. He's never let them down in the past. The corporate culture is that Bill's always right."[33]

~

Gates evokes loyalty, but he shows his appreciation for good performance by both words and action:

"When I was preparing to take my company public, I arranged to distribute an unusually large share of ownership to employees. It was a way of letting them know how much their performance mattered."[34]

On the other hand:

"The flip side of rewarding performance is making sure that employees who don't contribute are carefully managed or reassigned. Employees need to see that their peers are really strong and that if someone isn't carrying his or her weight, an adjustment will be made."[35]

~

It is said that each year Microsoft fires the weakest 5 percent of its programmers, thus keeping the staff fresh and strong. A Microsoft official points out, however, that employee turnover at Microsoft is still below the industry average.[36]

According to 1995 figures, the average departure rate for U.S. computer companies is 20.8 percent. For all U.S. companies, the rate is 16 percent. At Microsoft, the departure rate is 8.7 percent. Even that number is higher than Gates wants it to be:

> *"Our company is unusual in that most of the employees who are important to us are owners of the company and tend to have made a lot of money through our stock option plan. They tend to have the financial freedom not to work."[37]*

$\sim$

Although Gates may regret having left college, he doesn't see a business degree as necessary:

> *"Let me put it this way. Say you added two years to my life and let me go to business school. I don't think I would have done a better job at Microsoft. Let's look around these shelves and see if there are any business books. Oops. We didn't need any."[38]*

NEVER MIND THE GOOD NEWS— REPORT THE BAD

A product review meeting with Microsoft's CEO is called a BEC (Bill's Executive Committee) or a BOOP

(Bill's Office of the President). A BOOP can be harrowing, explains one employee:

"Oh, God. It's like going to a haunted house. Scary, but *fun*. Bill loves people who stand up to him. He hates yes people."[39]

~

Writer Fred Moody described what happened when he attended a product development meeting where Gates presided. His public relations escort told the gathered team that Moody would sit by quietly, so he could see how Gates interacts in meetings of this type. Everyone in the room—with the exception of Moody and Gates—burst into deafening laughter.

"The meeting began with a brief presentation by a visibly nervous engineer who got no more than 20 words into his presentation before Gates exploded. For an hour, he screamed, waved his arms, shouted, interrupted, delivered himself of cruel and sarcastic insults, and generally berated his charges, who kept trying bravely to make their points without sending him over the homicidal edge.

"'Yikes!' I thought. 'Isn't someone going to call the police?'

"Finally, the meeting ended with Gates sitting silently in his chair, rocking rhythmically back and forth, lost in thought. Then he said, quietly, 'OK . . . sounds good . . . go ahead.'"[40]

Gates later explained to Moody that prior to the meeting he'd read a lot of e-mail about the project, and he was just challenging the team to make sure they'd really thought everything through.

~

When Gates tells you that you've just said something stupid, it doesn't necessarily mean you're about to become part of that 8.7 percent annual employee attrition. Gates is so famous for telling staff that something is "the dumbest thing he ever heard" that even he has to make fun of himself:

> *"The world is full of superlative events. I reach new extremes. It's incredible. There's some kind of attenuation for past events, so I'm constantly running into the most stupid thing I've ever heard. Makes life fun! I know that my climaxes are ahead of me, not just behind me."[41]*

~

When Nathan Myhrvold first met Gates, he noticed an important quality:

"I was impressed that Bill was able to admit he was wrong. If someone has a better way or a better technology, Bill's very open to that."[42]

~

Raucous meetings aren't reserved just for employees:

The liaison between Microsoft and Intel has made both companies industry powerhouses. Gates and Grove were thrown together when IBM chose not to base an early PC on the 386 microprocessor, but Gates preferred the newer, more powerful chip. Other PC makers went along, which led to a loss of market share for IBM. Although Gates and Grove eventually became allies, they did not have an easy beginning. This is a portion of a joint interview published in *Fortune*:

> Gates: . . . at one point, I remember our Intel liaison didn't feel Microsoft was being, shall we say, responsive on a certain project. So I came to your house for a dinner. Our contractor was rolling you out as a big gun to put me in my place.
>
> Grove: It was not a pleasant evening. I remember the caterer peeked into the dining room to see what all the ruckus was about. I was the only one who finished my salmon.
>
> Gates: Yeah, we definitely had different views.
>
> Grove: After that, other people in our companies continued to do business, but the two of us didn't speak for quite some time.[43]

In recent years Grove and Gates have worked so closely together that they've become known as the Wintel Twins.[44]

~

In a 1990 video to employees, *Shipping Software*, Chris Peters told employees how best to work at Microsoft. The cardinal rule? Keep Bill informed:

"...you should never hide anything from Bill, because he's so good at knowing everything. But you should be firm, and you should yell back. The only recommendation I can bring or give you guys is to bring your very, very, very best developers with you to the meeting so they can quote things off the top of their head and they can just bury him with facts...Don't ever be unprepared. But say no. Bill respects no."[45]

～

While good news travels quickly through an organization with no special effort, Gates says there is a dangerous tendency to turn a blind eye toward bad news:

> *"To a certain extent, a little blindness is necessary when you undertake a risk. You have to have a little suspension of disbelief where you say, 'Hey, we're going to do this unproven product. Let's do our best.'*
>
> *"But every once in a while, some part of your organization needs to evaluate whether or not there really is a market for what's been undertaken. It's hard to do. Would you want to be the one to call the meeting to say that the whole thing's a dead end?"[46]*

～

Bad news, says Gates, can be acted upon.

> *"We never waste a lot of time talking about what we're doing well. It just isn't our culture. Every meeting is about 'Sure, we won in seven of the categories, but what about that eighth category?'"[47]*

Microsoft holds employee retreats, but Gates insists that they focus on work issues rather than be "mixers," or "team building exercises." They are held within a few hours of headquarters in Redmond, Washington, by car, and the first requirement is that the hotel have enough outgoing phone lines to let everyone connect their laptop computers to e-mail each evening. And employees are expected to put themselves on the firing line:

> *"We tell people that if no one laughs at at least one of their ideas, they're probably not being creative enough."*[48]

> *"I'm biased against conferences in exotic surroundings. It seems that the more attractive the location, the less work gets done."*[49]

An exception? Gates attends the World Economics Forum annually in Davos, Switzerland. Among the nearly 2,000 academics, politicians, and business leaders who have attended the conference are financier George Soros, Russian Prime Minister Viktor Chermomyrdin, and First Lady Hillary Clinton.

DON'T WASTE A THING—
ESPECIALLY TIME

Gates may spend $73 million on his house and $380,000 on an exotic Porsche, but he's conservative when it comes to business practices. For years he has flown coach on a commercial airline. Gates bought a corporate jet for personal and family use in 1997. On business trips he often still travels on commercial airlines in coach class, but when he must use his personal airplane, he does not bill Microsoft for the cost.

> *"It sets a good example. [Flying coach] costs less money. You get there just as fast as flying first-class. And my body fits. If I was really wide or really tall, I might view the issue differently. Because I travel about 14 weeks out of each year, airlines sometimes bump me up to first class even though I have a coach ticket. I don't resist when this happens."[50]*

However, on long night flights, Gates often wanders back to coach searching for an empty row where he can stretch out and sleep—much more comfortable than first class, he says.

∼

In 1992, when Gates was already a billionaire, his assistant complained that she was swamped and asked for more help. Gates responded: "Who am I? The Queen?"[51]

∼

Gates is as frugal with time as he is with money. From when he first started Microsoft, Gates was always in a hurry. If his airplane left at 10 A.M., he would leave the office at 9:50, racing to the airport and dashing onto the plane just as the door closed. He still hates wasting time:[52]

> *"For example, when I go to a meeting, I keep specific objectives in mind. There isn't much small talk, especially if I'm with colleagues I know well. We discuss accounts we lost or where overhead is too high, and then we're done. Bang! There are always more challenges than there are hours, so why be wasteful?"*[53]

~

Explained Charles Simonyi, one of Microsoft's best-known programmers: "Bill isn't going to explain everything twice."[54]

~

> *"Because there aren't enough hours in the day, it's tempting to try to do two things at once. Right now I'm perfecting reading a newspaper and riding an exercise bike at the same time—a very practical form of multitasking."*[55]

~

Gates says that because he now has a family, he no longer pulls all-night work sessions, catnapping during the day to get by. However:

> *"I envy people who thrive on three or four hours of sleep a night. They have so much more time to work, learn and play."*[56]

~

Gates's work style has been direct and simple from the time the company first started. He does not have a secretary in the old-fashioned sense, although he has an assistant who helps make arrangements, tracks him down when necessary, and handles many details when he's gone from the office:

"All of my electronic mail comes directly to me, and I answer it myself. I type all of my own memos and letters. In fact, I type a lot more words than the administrative assistant who sits outside my office."[57]

NOTE: When this author e-mailed Mr. Gates regarding this book, the director of corporate communications initially answered.

～

Steve Ballmer looks at Gates's calendar on a regular basis to help him decide if he's spending his time efficiently and focused on the right subjects. Gates explains:

"The products that comprise 80 percent of our revenue I choose to understand very, very deeply."[58]

～

To Gates, there is more to his frugality than just saving time and saving money:

"I like pushing things to the edge. That's often where you find high performance."[59]

～

64

WORK HARD/PLAY HARD

Bill Gates barreled onto the stage at one of Microsoft's annual employee meetings on a Harley-Davidson motorcycle as a revved-up crowd cheered.

While Microsofties often work up to 80-hour weeks, they also play hockey in the hallways, trick each other, play their musical instruments at work, plaster one another's offices shut, decorate their spaces in any way they choose, and have fun. The Microsoft campus in Redmond is like a massive college campus, dotted with soccer fields, basketball courts, and running paths.

To understand Microsoft, said one developer, you have to understand that we're all adolescents.[60] And proud of it.

～

In Microsoft's early days, Gates and Allen let off steam like the frisky kids they were. After a National Computer Conference in New York where the two put on a successful demonstration of Microsoft BASIC, a friend arrived at the Plaza Hotel on Central Park to find the partners shooting off fireworks from their hotel room window. Kay Nishi, Microsoft's Japanese representative, arrived with a group of clients, for whom he had neglected to book hotel rooms. That night 15 extra people stayed in the room, sleeping wherever they could find a space.

～

The Microgames, intense outdoor competitions based on the games the Gates family and their friends played at summer retreats, once were a tradition with the company. They are no longer held, but Microsoft Christmas parties have grown bigger and more flamboyant. Held at the Seattle Convention Center, even as early as 1990 more than 8,000 employees and guests attended. The theme that year was Holiday in Manhattan. Panhandlers and New York cops pestered the partygoers, who could visit the Little Italy deli, a faux Metropolitan Museum of Art, Broadway Lullaby Showroom, Blue Note Jazz Room, Hard Rock Café, or a Coney Island rumpus room for the children.[61]

E-CABULARY

The computer industry—and Microsoft in particular—has a vernacular of its own—often made up of high-tech similes and metaphors, acronyms, or speed-bump versions of long, complex descriptions of products or procedures. Electronic mail becomes e-mail. Here is an electronic glossary with a smattering of E-Cab.

Bandwidth: A human characteristic named after an electronic communications channel. Narrow bandwidth channels can't carry many messages at once, but a wide bandwidth channel processes a lot of information. Gates is a wide bandwidth person, good at "multitasking," or thinking clearly on several subjects simultaneously.

Big iron: Mainframe computer architecture, physically larger and with greater capabilities than personal computers, laptops, briefcase computers, palmtops, and so forth.

Bloatware: Software that grows ever larger and hogs space in a computer's memory.

Bogu: Years back, Microsoft programmers felt they had to take so much flak from IBM executives that they coined this code word for IBM meetings—"bend over and grease up." Later the word became "bogus," due to Steve Ballmer's deference to IBM—"bend over and grease up Steve."

Dislocation: Getting fired or being made obsolete. Dislocations are a certainty as the computer revolution and Internet expand.[62]

Drill down: Microspeak for getting deep into details.

FUD factor: Fear, uncertainty, and doubt—things that vaporware (see *Vaporware*) is intended to create among competitors.

Granularity: Fineness of detail or quality. As in "Microsoft Word is high granularity."

GUI or gooey: Graphical User Interface programs that allow the smooth blending of graphics and text, which was essential to the development of icon-based Windows software.

Hard core: Absolutely dedicated to a concept, principle, task, or company.

Massively parallel: Another Gatesian measure of I.Q. It refers to a setup where many independent microprocessors are linked in parallel to function as a problem-solving supercomputer. Gates thinks Myhrvold is massively parallel.

OEM: Original Equipment Manufacturer of components that are used in the assembly of name brands. For example, in a Compaq Computer with a Sony CD-ROM drive, the OEM for the drive is Sony.

OS: An Operating System, that is, a traffic manager that controls a computer and allows users to enter and run other programs. The OS in MS-DOS indicates it is an operating system.

Shovelware: Software where manufacturer's shovel in anything, regardless of its value. Originally CD-ROMs were called shovelware because so many junky ones were marketed, as the one entitled "The Complete History of Cows."

Softer software: Software that learns about you and anticipates your needs. For example, if your name has an unusual spelling, it will recognize that and put it in the spell checker correctly.

Vaporware: Software that is announced before it exists to mislead competitors into thinking they are too late in coming out with a new software program. See *FUD factor*.

Wreck a nice beach: The pet name of a Microsoft work group trying to teach computers to "recognize speech." The computer has trouble telling the difference between wrecking a nice beach and recognizing speech.[63]

THE MICROSOFT BUSINESS MODEL

MANAGING INNOVATION

> *"The entrepreneurial mind-set continues to thrive at Microsoft because one of our major goals is to reinvent ourselves—we have to make sure that we are the ones replacing our products instead of someone else."[1]*

The following Gates guidelines for managing new project developments are distilled from several sources:[2]

* Hire smart people:

> *" . . . software development still involves smart engineers thinking through algorithms and typing them out. Success still involves getting people to work together, and bringing expertise to testing. There have been many quantitative changes. But the character of building software, and the kinds of people who are good at it, haven't changed at all."[3]*

Greg Maffei, Microsoft vice president and chief financial officer says, "This is a company with an enormous amount of intellectual challenge. It's like drinking from a fire hose."[4]

* Allow unicycles. If you seek creative products, you must encourage an atmosphere of creativity:[5]

"Software is a great combination between artistry and engineering. When you finally get done and get to appreciate what you have, it is like a part of yourself that you've put together."[6]

~

"If you ever talk to a great programmer, you'll find he knows his tools like an artist knows his paintbrushes."[7]

* Work with small teams. Microsoft often limits its work teams to 35 people:

"As the company has grown, we have continually worked to have an organization within an organization. Small teams can communicate efficiently and aren't encumbered by a big structure slowing them down."[8]

~

"You need a strong team, because a mediocre team gives mediocre results, no matter how well managed it is."[9]

~

* Give people time to think:

    "People must have time to think about things."[10]

* Make quick decisions and stick with them:

Nathan Myhrvold says speed is essential. "A revenue-generating franchise is the most fragile thing in the world. No matter how good your product, you are only 18 months away from failure."[11]

~

Gates says:

> *"Don't make the same decision twice. Spend time and thought to make a solid decision the first time so that you don't revisit the issue unnecessarily. If you're too willing to reopen issues, it interferes not only with your execution but also with your motivation to make a decision in the first place. After all, why bother deciding an issue if it isn't really decided?"*[12]

* Develop a fast feed-back loop, especially with customers:

    "Microsoft is a company that moves very rapidly, and we set priorities based on what our customers are asking for."[13]

    ~

    "I like question and answer periods because they allow me to get a sense of what people are excited about and what they are upset about."[14]

* Learn from past projects. [15]

Microsoft gleaned an important lesson from the "mail merge couch":

> *"The early version of Mail Merge was so compli-cated that whenever a customer called for help, our representative would lie down on the couch to take the call, knowing the conversations was likely to last a long time. Clearly something was wrong."[16]*

Although it strives to learn from past mistakes, Mike Murray, Microsoft's vice president of human resources and administration, describes the company this way: "If Microsoft were a car, it would have a large gas pedal and a small but workable brake. It would not have a rear view mirror."[17]

* Critics have said that Microsoft is quick to spot good work by others and convert it for its own use. Microsoft officials say their company does not con-vert technology, though Gates says Microsoft does embrace and extend that which is new:

> *"Our great successes come with an approach of embracing anything that's popular and then coming along with extensions. That's the approach that worked for us with NetWare, the approach that worked in spreadsheets and word processing, with the Internet— to embrace everything that's out there and make it easy for systems to co-exist."[18]*

~

"In a fast-moving industry, the companies that are successful are those that are able to get out in the front of the key trends and really add value in the new applications."[19]

* Never give up:

Steve Ballmer says persistence is critically important: "It doesn't matter if we bang our heads and fail. We keep right on banging and banging and banging and banging and banging."[20]

* Use every talent:

Microsoft has been so successful because Gates is both a technician and a businessman.

"I think the success of Microsoft has come from knowing these things have a relationship with each other. The two sides drive each other."[21]

~

In Gates's mind, business management isn't all that difficult:

"I think business is very simple. Profit. Loss. Take the sales, subtract the costs, you get this big positive number. The math is quite straightforward."[22]

~

Internet jokers have their own view of Microsoft's business principles:

> *Question:* How many Microsoft vice presidents does it take to change a light bulb?
> *Answer:* Eight; one to work the bulb and seven to make sure Microsoft gets $2 for every light bulb ever changed anywhere in the world.

MICROSOFT ABROAD

Microsoft has sales offices in nearly 60 countries and an international staff of 6,200. Almost all of the employees are natives of the countries in which they work. It is estimated that each overseas employee generates more than $1 million in annual revenues. Gates says he tries to make certain that his foreign partners are in charge and that they share in the wealth:

> *"That's key. It sends the wrong message to have a foreigner come in to run things."[23]*

$$\sim$$

> *"You've probably noticed our share [of Internet Explorer 4.0] is a little bit higher outside the United States than inside the United States. That's true for virtually every product Microsoft offers. Our competitors are relatively less competent at doing business outside the United States than inside the United States, so we always manage to do very well. In fact, the worst thing that we can say to a sub-*

*sidiary is that their share is the same as it is in the
United States."*[24]

In Japan, for example, Microsoft has partnerships
with at least 28 different software and hardware manufacturers.[25]

~

When Microsoft sponsored a 1998 seminar for governments that use Microsoft products, about 300 representatives of 71 world governments attended.

~

About 80 million PCs are sold each year, 50 million of
them outside the United States.

~

Gates travels endlessly, visiting Europe, South Africa,
India, and China. A 1997 trip to India and South Africa
involved almost 25,000 miles of travel, 14 formal
speeches, more than three dozen personal meetings
and presentations.

The lesser-developed countries are key:

*"That's where we'll get a lot of our growth in the
coming years. These countries are only just getting
started buying PCs in big numbers. And because
they usually don't have lots of legacy systems
already in place—you know, mainframes and mini-
computers—we have a chance to have an even bigger share of the overall computer business than we*

do in the U.S. or Europe or Japan. You bet I think it's important."[26]

~

Gates learns much about the needs of overseas customers in his travels abroad.

"I never realized that there are 14 distinct written and spoken languages in India. Now that I understand that, we're going to invest a whole lot more in localizing our products. And the raw software talent there really grabs you. A billion people is a lot of people, and even though the country is really poor, there are a lot of talented people with world-class educations, and companies that are as forward-looking and capable as anywhere. I came back quite enthused about taking some of our software development overload here and moving it over there."[27]

~

"India holds tremendous potential of becoming a software superpower, provided the government matches the human skills with the required infrastructure."[28]

~

"The growing technical prowess of nations such as India unnerves some people in developed countries who fear a loss of jobs and opportunities. I think these fears are misplaced. Economics is not a zero-sum game."[29]

~

Gates's travel schedule is grueling. Following his 1997 visit to Davos, Switzerland, to meet with world leaders, Gates made this four-day sprint through Europe:

Day 1: Flew to Paris to meet with brass of PSA/Citroën to conclude an agreement to use Microsoft Auto PC technology.

Delivered keynote speech at Comdex in Porte de Versailles City.

Day 2: To Brussels, Belgium, where Gates met with Prince Philippe and the Federation of Belgian Companies.

Met with Prime Minister Jean-Luc Dehaene and his cabinet to discuss infrastructure.

Spoke at Microsoft's New Technology Summit.

Met with officials from schools that use information technology in innovative ways.

Closed the day with a speech to Flemish education leaders.

Day 3: On to Helsinki, Finland, to deliver the keynote speech at a seminar for 800 Finnish business leaders.

Flew to Stockholm, Sweden, to meet with Prime Minister Goran Persson.

Addressed a Stockholm seminar hosted by Microsoft.

Spoke in Kammarsalen at the launch of Microsoft's new Nordic division.

Day 4: Last day. Flew to Munich, Germany, to meet with the president of Siemens AG, one of the world's largest technology companies, to cement relations between Microsoft and Siemens.

Made a video teleconference speech to a Deutsche Telekom group in Hanover.

Delivered a speech at a BMW/Deutsche Bank workshop on technology.

Met with Dr. Edmound Stroiber, president of the state of Bavaria.

Summation: Visited five countries, met one prince and four heads of government, delivered eight speeches, opened a foreign office, and confirmed two major corporate agreements—in four days.[30]

～

The antitrust dispute between Microsoft and the U.S. government is being waged at a time when the globalization of business is forcing a reexamination of domestic attitudes regarding economic monopolies. The fact that 55 percent of Microsoft's business is overseas at a time when U.S. trade deficits are rocketing has made it more difficult for the Justice Department to suppress the company's activities.

～

Computers and the Internet, Gates says, will spread wealth and power more evenly around the globe:

"In early human history, technological advantages were built on the availability of certain plants, animals, and geographies.

"In today's emerging information society, the critical natural resources are human intelligence, skill, and leadership. Every region of the world has these in abundance, which promises to make the next chapter of human history particularly interesting."[31]

THE ACQUISITION POLICY

By late 1997 Microsoft had made about 60 acquisitions, investments, or alliances worth more than $2.5 billion. Ten companies were bought in 1997, making Microsoft the leader in software acquisitions. In addition, Microsoft has smaller investment positions in dozens of other enterprises.

Charles Federman, chairman of Broadview Associates, a mergers and acquisitions advisor, says, "I see no other company in this industry that is moving as aggressively and with as singular a purpose."[32]

∼

Gates's vision for the future drives his acquisition strategy. He fears that infrastructure and computer hardware will not keep pace with innovations and improvement in software:

"I do worry about getting the bandwidth, not only to businesses, but into the home. So we did a number of

things. We invested in Comcast [a cable access company] to help them accelerate it."[33]

∼

Gates encourages telephone companies to provide Internet services, but also:

"I personally invested in this satellite scheme [Teledesic Corporation] which will provide good connectivity to rural areas. In cities you might as well run the fiber, as it's the most economic thing, but when you get out where you don't have that kind of population density, it won't be economic to run the fibers, and that's where a low orbit satellite approach could come in and give you the same very high-speed connectivity to every point of the globe. [Microsoft is] not in the delivery business. We're not going to buy fibers or communications companies because that's not our expertise, but we're going to do everything we can to help drive that forward."[34]

∼

Sun Microsystems' Scott McNealy sees danger in Microsoft's wide-ranging acquisitions: "As Microsoft seeks to leverage its current monopolies into large business computers, broadcasting, entertainment, newspapers, cable TV, travel services, Internet services, database software, home banking, and so on . . . It has power that IBM, even at its zenith, never had."[35]

When *Business Week* magazine suggested that he was becoming a news-media mogul, Gates squirmed in his chair and screwed up his face:

> *"The notion that Microsoft is a media company is a strange thing to say."[36]*

Perhaps not so strange: Microsoft Press publishes books. The product portfolio of Microsoft's interactive media group includes the Microsoft Network, MSNBC, and a wide range of educational, informational, and entertainment CD-ROM titles including the encyclopedia Encarta. In January 1998 more than 270,000 readers logged on to Microsoft's on-line magazine, *Slate*, at www.slate.com.

Gates personally bought the Otto Bettmann library of drawings, photographs, and other illustrations for his Corbis Corporation.

BILL LABS

Smithsonian magazine asked Bill Gates if he could visit any moment from the past, what would it be? He chose to witness the invention of the transistor at Bell Labs in December 1947:

> *"It was a key transitional event in the advent of the Information Age. It supplanted the vacuum tube and enabled the concept of electronic devices on a personal scale. Some of us still remember how cool it felt*

*to be able to carry your own transistor radio around
and listen to whatever music you wanted, wherever
you were."*[37]

The transistor was soon made obsolete by the integrated circuit; nevertheless it was a preliminary step toward the invention of the personal computer.

～

Microsoft spends more than $2 billion a year on research and development because Gates knows that every product the company sells will be obsolete within a few years:

*"At Microsoft, we take the long-term view. That
means we invest a lot in research and development to
help us understand future directions, while staying
competitive in terms of product development today.
It's obviously a big challenge for any company to
remain vital and to successfully transition to new
business models as needed."*[38]

～

*"We come into work every day knowing that we can
destroy the company . . . and that we better keep our
wits about us, make the long-term investments in
research that are going to make a big difference and
really drive things forward."*[39]

～

*"This is a scale-of-economics business where the
marginal costs of selling an extra copy of software*

is very small, so we can afford to put billions into the R&D of these products that go out to a large mass market."[40]

~

Some research will be conducted abroad:

" . . . we are building up a number of development centers around the world. We're in Israel. We're in China. We're starting to build some things in India. The research group wanted to make sure that they were drawing on all the great research going on around the world."[41]

~

Cambridge, England, is a typical overseas research location:

"The key is the quality of the university systems, and turning out lots of [information technology] graduates that can do very strong work."[42]

~

At a speech at St. John's College, Cambridge, Gates said:

"With a research lab you don't want to sit at a press conference and say, 'In three years they will invent the following ten things.' Part of the beauty of research is getting the greatest minds together without any deadline.

"They are allowed to look into these areas and make more fundamental advances than the product

groups who have those deadlines to make. We are not going to make hard-core predictions, but it's safe to say that the close relationships we form between our researchers and product groups have already shown we can move the great ideas as they come along without a schedule into the products."[43]

~

Although Gates does not know what exact future benefits will accrue from Microsoft's research efforts, he expects some commercial gain. He doesn't want Microsoft to be like Xerox:

"The work done at the Xerox Palo Alto Research Center [PARC] is the source of the basic approach to personal computing that's popular today. But it's certainly a cautionary tale from a business point of view that all investment and all that work was done, and Xerox was never able to take advantage of that. I don't think it's something that's necessary. If you do the right things, you get the people working together the right way, there's no better investment than great research work."[44]

~

Some professional organizations for engineers have protested that U.S. high-tech companies are laying off American engineers. High-tech companies either export their businesses to other countries where it can be done less expensively, or bring foreign engineers to this country who will work for lower salaries.

In 1995 Gates protested a proposed change in the immigration law that might limit the number of engineers and technical people who could move to the United States for employment:

"As it happens, only about 5 percent of our U.S.-based software developers come from outside the United States, but its absolutely critical that we have an environment in which great minds from many countries can work together. We rely on skilled foreign workers for their math, science, and creative abilities as well as their cultural knowledge, which helps when localizing products for world markets."[45]

~

There is also a "Paul Labs." Paul Allen established a $100-million think tank called Interval Research, hoping to help shape the Information Highway.

THE COMPUTER WARS

BATTLING PIRATES

Bill Gates was the first person to object to the pirating of software and explain that the industry would go nowhere unless computer users paid programmers for their work.

Gates often took part in the MITS Mobile Caravan, a road show that traveled the country demonstrating the Altair computer to hobbyists. At the Homebrew Computer Club in Palo Alto, California, someone accidentally dropped the punch tape for the BASIC program on the floor. A club member grabbed up the tape and gave it to member Dave Sokol to copy. Sokol duplicated the tape and handed out free copies at the club's next meeting.

Gates soon realized that computer users everywhere were freely copying disks and giving away BASIC software to others. In 1975 Gates fired off a letter to the *Computer Notes* newsletter. In his "Open Letter to Hobbyists," Gates accused the hobbyists of thievery.

"As the majority of hobbyists must be aware, most of you steal your software. Hardware must be paid for, but software is something to share. Who cares if the people who worked on it get paid?"[1]

～

Gates was chastized by Ed Roberts, the manufacturer of the Altair 8080, for the scathing letter. Gates wrote a second letter toning things down a little, but his fiery reaction sparked a nationwide furor over piracy. Software soon became recognized as a copyrighted product, and it became unacceptable in computer circles to use appropriated software. Nevertheless, the problem of pirated software continues to bedevil the computer industry.

Ironically, the widespread sharing of BASIC software made it the standard language of microcomputers.

～

Although software pirating in Asia and Latin America is a particularly serious problem, pirating occurs everywhere. In January of 1998 Microsoft filed a dozen lawsuits against computer resellers in New York City, Boston, and San Francisco, claiming that they installed unlicensed software and distributed counterfeit Microsoft products.

～

It is estimated that 68 percent of the software used in Brazil was illegally obtained. In 1997 Microsoft cut a $10-million deal with the Brazilian government to supply PC software to 300,000 public schools. In return, the Brazilian government will ask teachers to use only legal software. Microsoft hopes to stem the flow of pirated software by education, establishing precedents, and setting good examples. "In the past, you'd have a bunch of cowboys going around the world threatening people," says Orlando Ayala, Microsoft's vice president of international operations. "That's not the way to do it."[2]

In November 1997 Gates met with Philippines President Fidel Ramos in the United States, and signed a pact to help that country develop a long-term information technology plan and create national Internet sites for education and government uses. In turn, the Philippines pledged to protect Microsoft's intellectual property rights through laws and their enforcement.[3]

Following the signing, Gates gave Ramos a certificate legalizing much of the government's pirated Microsoft software. The government would be able to buy newer software at half price. Gates said he would visit the Philippines sometime in 1998.

The Argentine Supreme Court landed a blow to software makers in 1998 when it handed down a decision that virtually legalized software piracy in that country. It is estimated that royalties were not paid on roughly 71 percent of the software used there, the main abusers being small private companies and local and federal government agencies. Lost revenues on Microsoft Word alone were estimated at $165 million.[4]

~

Gates expects that eventually, even countries like China that now resist will enforce antipiracy laws:

> *"Countries, as they get more developed, want to foster a local software industry, so they pass laws and do better and better."*[5]

BATTLING COMPETITORS

The computer industry is such a tangled web of cooperation and competition that Andy Grove, chairman of Intel, titled his book *Only the Paranoid Survive*. For example, Sun Microsystems, while battling both Microsoft and Hewlett-Packard for undermining its Java "write once–use anywhere" language, strengthened its alliance with Intel. At the same time, Microsoft and Intel continued to build their long, strong business relationship.

There is a constant swarm of lawsuits over ownership, appropriation, copyright, and similar issues—and the stakes are high. A popular software program may earn many millions of dollars.

~

Randall Stross, writing in *U.S. News & World Report*:

"It's frightening how one software company so dominates its market, isn't it? Company No. 2 is so far behind, it's nothing less than pathetic. And how is any other company ever going to have a chance of catching up with the front-runner, which—under the banner of helping set 'industry standards'—continually cooks up new variations of its own proprietary technology?"[6]

But Stross didn't mean Microsoft. He was writing about Netscape, the company that accused *Microsoft* of being a monopolist when it entered Netscape's territory of Internet browsers. About a year after Stross wrote this, Microsoft gained ground on Netscape and captured nearly half of the market.[7]

∿

Events often take an ironic twist. Jim Barksdale, chief executive of Netscape Communications, testified before Congress that Microsoft was being unfair. "We have been under very serious pressure. They have successfully made [Microsoft Explorer] a free product," said Barksdale.[8]

Just a year earlier *GQ* magazine described how Marc Andreeson, the young legend behind Netscape's browser software, had done the reverse. As a student, Andreeson helped develop software at the University of Illinois to be used free by academics and scientists. He then wrote and commercialized a slightly different version for Netscape. Both Andreeson and Barksdale became millionaires.[9]

∿

Mitchell Kapor, former head of Lotus Development, explained the personal computer business this way: "The PC business is *war*. Either you fight or you're a casualty. You have to look the enemy in the eye and never, ever blink."[10]

NOTE: Kapor's comment comes from the book *Start-Up: A Silicon Valley Adventure*, in which author Jerry Kaplan claimed his fledgling Go Corporation failed due to anticompetitive practices by both Microsoft *and* IBM.

∼

Gates is constantly on the offensive:

> *"You always have to be thinking about who is coming to get you."[11]*

∼

In its earlier years, Microsoft was seen as a scrappy underdog in the computer world. In due time, it became the big dog. Now when a software company grows big, it risks attracting the attention of Microsoft, complained *Business Week*:

"The giant is legendary for the way it targets a rival, dissects is strengths and weaknesses, then finds a way to devour its market. Think about Borland, Lotus, WordPerfect, and Novell. Each was mighty in its day, but they were hobbled after Microsoft set its sights on them."[12]

∼

What catapulted Microsoft from little guy to leader? According to Gates, it was ideas:

"We had ideas that the giants of the time missed. We're always thinking about what we have missed that could keep us on top."[13]

∽

In high-tech circles, neither friends nor enemies are permanently so:

In 1988 Apple Computers sued Microsoft over Windows 2.03 claiming Microsoft stole the "look and feel" of its graphical interface product. Microsoft won the lawsuit, and for years Microsoft and Apple were considered mortal enemies. Yet *Los Angeles Times* computer columnist Charles Piller has a different opinion:

"Microsoft is perfectly happy to collect huge profits from Mac applications—as demonstrated by its recent commitment to develop Mac Office for five years, and its $150 million investment in Apple. And as much as the industry still needs Apple as a spurt to innovation and to keep the concept of [IBM's] OS competition alive, Gates likes Apple as a hedge against further action by the Justice Department."[14]

∽

In 1997 consumer advocate Ralph Nader organized an anti-Microsoft conference in Washington, D.C. When Gates turned down an invitation to speak, Nader accused him of "refusing to address the issues raised at the conference . . . He is still in virtual reality and out of touch with what is the growing public challenge to his company's power abuses and intimidations."[15]

Gates claimed that the attackers were motivated by self-interest and that he wouldn't take the attacks passively:

> *"We do have some competitors who have chosen to fund these things and promote these activities in order to handicap Microsoft in the competitive market."[16]*

~

Strange bedfellows to consumer advocate Ralph Nader, Bob Dole, former U.S. Senator and Republican presidential candidate, and former conservative Supreme Court candidate Robert Bork, joined the attack on Microsoft. Late in 1997 Dole sent out letters seeking the support of corporate America in a campaign to curb Microsoft's Internet business. Dole's Washington, D.C., law firm, Verner Liipfert Bernhard McPherson & Hand, represented Netscape Communications, Sun Microsystems, and other competitors.

"In the coming months, we will need to educate the public, the administration, and Congress about the dangers of a laissez-faire attitude toward Microsoft. I am personally convinced that if nothing is done now, it will become increasingly difficult to have fair competition in the years ahead," Dole explained.

"As you know, I have never been an advocate of overly aggressive antitrust enforcement. I am nonetheless convinced that, if we are to maintain a competitive electronic marketplace, we must enforce our existing antitrust laws to ensure that no one company dominates the Internet and access to it," he added.[17]

Former judge Bork was hired by Netscape to help further that company's interest in protecting its browser from Microsoft competition.

~

"It's not just our lunch, but our carcasses, that Microsoft wants to eat," said Gary Reback, a Silicon Valley lawyer representing Sun Microsystems and others.[18]

~

Gates hired his own Washington lobbyists and fought back:

> *"You'll see us speaking back in terms of asking people to look at what motivates these attacks and what's really behind them."[19]*

Gates also asked that Microsoft be recognized for its positive contribution to the development of technology:

> *" . . . because this is not a country where success and great products should be punished."[20]*

~

Steve Ballmer, Microsoft's number two in command, does not deny that Microsoft is a tough competitor. "I wouldn't call 'sensitive' a birth attribute of Microsoft, or even of Microsoft's senior management," Ballmer admitted. But, "In a world in which we are perceived of as being powerful, I don't think we can make bad business decisions, but there might be ways of being more benevolent."[21]

∼

Microsoft can take credit for keeping other companies on their toes. There is a computer industry saying: "Either fix your problems or just send all your money to Bill."[22]

∼

Despite Gates's assurance that Microsoft has no interest in dominating the field, cable television executives are concerned that interactive television, set-top boxes, and other technology will let Gates get a hold on the cable TV industry.

Ted Turner, vice chairman of media conglomerate Time Warner, noted, "Any time you have too much power in any one place, it's not healthy for anybody . . . But we're not about to let one maker of hardware or software get in and control everything. This industry will not allow for a closed system. If we do, we should all just turn over our future to Microsoft."

Nevertheless, Turner later conceded that the cable industry would change and: "The smart money is gonna rise, and the dumb asses are gonna fall by the wayside."[23]

∼

While Microsoft was being attacked by competitors and the U.S. Justice Department as anti-competitive, it tied for second place with the Swiss company ABB for most respected company in the world. General Electric won first place in the 1996 *Financial Times* poll of chief executives.[24]

JAVA, JAVA, JING-JING-JING

Sun Microsystems and Microsoft had an agreement allowing Microsoft to adapt the Java language to the Windows and NT platforms. However, when Microsoft's NT product was released, it was not compatible with Sun's versions of Java. In other words, NT's Java did not allow programmers to "write once—use anywhere," as the language was intended to do. Sun sued, claiming Microsoft had violated its licensing agreement.[25] Microsoft filed a countersuit, and says that Sun is trying to use the courts to re-write a contract with Microsoft.

Sun Microsystems attorney Bruce Kerr moonlights writing parody jingles for "The Dr. Demento Show," Rush Limbaugh, and Bay Area radio and television stations. "Loose Bruce" wrote the following ditty to the tune of "Ja-da," a popular World War I song:

"Bill said, 'Hey, my recipe is richer than yours.' Scott said, 'I own the coffee pot, sit down and I'll pour.'

"Pour Java, Java, Java, Java, jing-jing-jing [the sound of a cash register]. Java, Java, Java Java jing-jing-jing. Nobody can tell yet what the future may bring. All we know is Java goes jing-jing-jing [cash register]."[26]

I AM HUMBLE, RESPECTFUL

The winter of 1997–98 was the winter of siege, as far as Bill Gates and Microsoft were concerned. Anti-Microsoft fever was flogged by Washington, D.C., lobbyists hired by Microsoft's competitors. The original antitrust investigation that started in 1993 accelerated and the U.S. Justice Department eyed Microsoft's every action. Due to Justice's objection, in 1995 Microsoft dropped its $2.1-million offer to buy software-maker Intuit. Now Justice was reviewing Microsoft's 1997 $150-million investment in Apple Computer.

On top of that, the Justice Department dragged Microsoft back into court in 1996, saying that the company twisted, tortured, and defied a 1995 order to offer computer makers Windows 95 software separate from the company's Internet Explorer Web browser.

Claiming the Justice Department's order crippled Windows, Microsoft gave its customers three choices. PC makers could delete Internet Explorer files from Windows 95, even though Microsoft warned that doing so could render the operating system useless; they could ship the PCs with an outdated, nearly three-year-old version of Windows that lacked the browser; or they could ship the latest version of Windows with Internet Explorer, for the same price.

The Justice Department was outraged.

"Microsoft's naked attempt to defeat the purpose of the court order and to further its litigation strategy is an affront to the court's authority," said department lawyer Joel Klein. "Microsoft has gone from tying its products to tying the hands of its vendors. The more Microsoft continues this practice, the more consumers are harmed."[27]

While it is not illegal to hold a monopoly, it is illegal to "tie," or to link, a new product to the monopoly product, then require clients to buy one if they buy the other.

~

An angry Gates characterized the government's scrutiny of Microsoft as "a witch hunt."[28]

Suddenly bureaucrats, journalists, television commentators, and stand-up comedians everywhere began portraying Gates as arrogant and unreasonable.

"Republicans have been claiming that Janet Reno was afraid to take on the world's most powerful man," said comedian Russ Myers. "Unfortunately, it looks like she thought they meant Bill Gates."[29]

~

Many people sided with Justice and felt Microsoft would not lose industry leadership if it complied with the court order.

"A company with Microsoft's skill should be able to produce two reasonable up-to-date versions of Windows—one with Internet Explorer, one without," wrote Amy Cortese, *Business Week* software editor. Given a choice, said Cortese, most makers would choose the Windows with the integrated Explorer. "All the government is asking, for now, is that PC makers and consumers get a choice. So, Bill, let the markets decide, and save yourself a lot of trouble."[30]

⌇

Though Gates was often portrayed as defiant and arrogant to the Justice Department, he says that impression was false:

> *"When your own government sues you, it's not a pleasant experience. I wasn't sitting there going 'ha, ha, ha, I'll do what I want.' I was thinking this is the worst thing that's ever happened to me."[31]*

⌇

> *"I am the opposite of defiant. I am disappointed. I am humble. I am respectful."[32]*

NOTE: For Microsoft's full point of view please refer to www.microsoft.com/corpinfo/doj/timeline.htm.

⌇

Eventually Microsoft complied with the judge's order to ship the Windows 95 operating system without forcing vendors to display Microsoft's software for browsing the Internet.

"Bill Gates finally understood he made a huge strategic and public-relations blunder in the way the company tried to respond to the judge's order," said Sam Miller, a San Francisco attorney who was involved in an earlier case involving Microsoft and the federal government. "It finally sank in that their arrogance backfired."[33]

Dean Katz, group public relations manager at Microsoft, explained his company's point of view this way in an e-mail to the author. "It wasn't that Microsoft 'finally complied' with the judge's order. We believed we had complied to the letter of the judge's order all along. However, Microsoft and DOJ disagreed on this point and we wanted to move beyond the disagreement, so we reached a temporary agreement with the government in which we offered computer makers two additional Windows 95 licensing options in addition to the three we had originally offered," Katz wrote.

∼

Gates apparently realized he had to sell his case to the public. He e-mailed *Business Week* explaining Microsoft's greater visibility in the nation's capital:

> *"We want to increase our dialogue with political leaders so they understand the excellence we stand for."*[34]

∼

Gates testified before Senator Orrin Hatch's Judiciary Committee. *Barron's* newspaper described hearings on Microsoft's business practices as a "ritual flogging" and noted that Gates "was not the argumentative, dismissive, hyperactive, hot-tempered Bill Gates of legend."[35]

∼

Despite those acts of contrition, Gates didn't back down:

"What you have here is, basically, the U.S. government saying our products are too capable . . . They're trying to get us not to support the Internet in Microsoft Windows. It's pretty straightforward. Yes, it's surprising, but it's pretty straightforward. So I'll tell my lawyers to defend our ability to do Windows 95, to do Windows NT, to do speech recognition. Observers of the legal process may or may not get confused about what goes on there, but I have asked them to defend that, because I think it's not only important for Microsoft—I think it's important for users of personal computers."[36]

~

"It's interesting where you have the Department of Justice asking in one of their filings to have a review process that they have to look over any new product that we do. And that really sounds a lot like product regulation."[37]

~

Gates insists that Microsoft is not a monopolist:

"As you know, a monopolist, by definition, is a company that has the ability to restrict entry by new firms and unilaterally control price. Microsoft can do neither."[38]

NOTE: The number of U.S. software businesses is growing rather than shrinking. *Fortune* magazine reported that in 1997, there were 2,200 software companies in the Boston area alone, compared to 600 in 1989. How many of these companies are in direct competition with Microsoft products or are beholden to play by rules set by Microsoft, however, is not known.[39]

~

"Antitrust is supposed to look for areas of the economy where a lack of competition is causing prices to go up and there [seems] to be no innovation, and yet here we have more money going into software start-ups than ever before. You go down to California and everybody's driving Ferraris—not everybody, but you know, it's like on trees down there."[40]

~

"The price of the operating system is 5 percent of the cost of the PC today. If I had a monopoly, the price of the operating system would be 25 to 35 percent of the price of the machine."[41]

~

"This is capitalism. We create a product called Windows. Who decides what's in Windows? It's the customers who buy Windows."[42]

~

"I think the government should be extremely wary of interceding in an industry like computer software that is working well on its own."[43]

~

"The PC industry is the model industry in the entire economy. The rate of innovation, the openness—all of these things are just fantastic. And Microsoft's role in creating this has been absolutely fundamental."[44]

~

Michael Morris, Sun Microsystems attorney, disagreed:

"Everybody's scared of Microsoft," said Morris. "The degree of reluctance on the part of people over whom Microsoft has huge commercial power to complain about Microsoft's behavior to government agencies is extraordinary. It's so well known in the valley, it's taken for granted. It's based on their ability to hurt companies—it's a matter of common knowledge."[45]

~

"Everybody hates a monopoly unless they've got one," said Netscape Communications chairman James Barksdale.[46]

~

Microsoft also has been under fire abroad. Japanese regulators followed the lead of the U.S. Justice Department and in 1997 began investigating Microsoft, as did European Union antitrust authorities. After discussions with the European Union, Microsoft agreed to renegotiate its software licensing agreements.

~

Even *Saturday Night Live* took a shot:

Bill Gates testified before the Senate recently insisting that Microsoft is not a monopoly. "He then hopped into a giant shoe and drove to his red hotel on Baltic Avenue."[47]

~

There are dozens of stories in the media and on the street about companies that have suffered at the hands of Microsoft, but the software giant also has advocates:

Robert Hall, a Stanford University economist who worked on the Microsoft case at one time, says, "We shouldn't be trying to stop Microsoft from putting more function into Windows—and you don't want to punish success."[48]

Defenders of Microsoft often compare this case to the 13-year Justice Department investigation of IBM. On January 31, 1969, the last working day in office of the Johnson administration, the government filed suit accusing IBM of monopolizing the U.S. computer industry. Three subsequent administrations pursued the company. In 1982 under the Reagan administration, Justice finally dropped the case.

~

Charles Munger, Warren Buffett's long-time partner and vice chairman of Berkshire Hathaway Inc., says the Justice Department made a mistake pursuing antitrust charges against Microsoft:

"If I were running the Justice Department," said Munger, who is an attorney, "the lawsuit would not have been filed. I've watched the leading industries in the United States, one after another, lose their shirts to clever foreigners. Now we have a company that is really winning big. The idea that we would weaken what is winning big around the world because it is hard on competitors here seems wrong. I can't think of anything more obvious than that software ought to be integrated well. I don't mean there won't always be other software that is used as a 'tack-on' system, but I don't want the airliners to be tacked together by 400 different suppliers. I like the idea that Boeing integrates the package. I'm strongly against what Justice is doing."[49]

～

On a visit to the Tech Museum in San Jose, Gates posed for snapshots at the request of the museum's high school interns. Afterward, one of the interns said she was sorry about a speech she gave at school describing Microsoft as a dangerous monopoly. "After seeing him," said 16-year-old Vicky Hoang, "I take it all back."[50]

～

The Microsoft Internet browser got Gates in trouble, but during the ordeal, the Internet access was his friend:

"In one weekend, I can sit at my PC, collaborate with attorneys all over the world, comment on a 48-page legal brief and e-mail it to the Department of Justice."[51]

～

Gates's efforts to appease the Justice Department failed. On May 18, 1998, the DOJ and 20 states filed antitrust lawsuits against Microsoft. Attorney General Janet Reno charged that the company had a "chokehold" on the market for Internet software, and illegally used its monopoly power to limit consumer choice. By June, the Federal Trade Commission and the Justice Department were investigating both chip maker and long-time Microsoft partner, Intel, in an effort to free up competition in both the computer software and hardware industries.[52]

~

Despite the seriousness of the situation, *Slate* on-line magazine published a humorous (though fictitious) letter from Gates to its advice columnist Prudence:

"I am just a guy named Bill being pursued by a gal named Janet. Janet was also pursuing another guy named Bill, but he somehow or other put her off the scent. She's stopped chasing him, but she's still chasing me! Neither of us appreciate her attentions. What I want to know is, why does she have this vendetta against guys named Bill? And how did the other one manage to lose her? What has he got that I don't got? Is life unfair, or what?"[53]

~

When asked if his antitrust problems would make him gun-shy of competing aggressively in the future, Gates replied: "... for me to become gun-shy might require surgery."[54]

NOTE: To read the government side of the Microsoft/ web browser story, log on to the Justice Department Web site, http://www.usdoj.gov.

~ ✳ ~

BILL BUYS AMERICAN—
OOPS, MAKE THAT AMERICA

Several versions of this fake memo circulated on the
Internet. One announced that Gates had bought the Cath-
olic church. In this one, Gates bought the entire United
States:

SUBJECT: *Microsoft Announces Major Acquisition*
Redmond, Washington, Oct. 21, 1997

In direct response to accusations made by the Department of Justice, Microsoft Corporation announced today
it will acquire the federal government of the United
States of America for an undisclosed sum. "It's actually
a logical extension of our growth," said Microsoft chairman and CEO Bill Gates. "It's a positive arrangement
for everyone."

Gates held a briefing at the Oval Office with U.S.
President Bill Clinton and assured the press that
changes to U.S. government policy will be minimal.

The United States will be managed as a wholly-
owned subsidiary of Microsoft Corp.

An initial public offering is planned for July 4 of
next year, and the federal government is expected to
be profitable by 1999, according to Microsoft President
Steve Ballmer.

Clinton said that he had "willingly and enthusiasti-
cally" accepted a position as vice president of USA
Operations with Microsoft and would continue to manage the U.S. government, reporting directly to Gates.

When asked how it felt to give up the mantle of
executive authority, Clinton said it was "a relief." He

added that Gates has a "proven track record" and that U.S. citizens should offer Gates their "full support and confidence."

In his new role at Microsoft, Clinton will earn several times the $200,000 a year he currently earns as U.S. president. Gates dismissed a rumor that the U.S. capitol would be moved to Redmond as "silly," though he said he would make executive decisions for the U.S. government from his existing office at Microsoft headquarters.

Gates said that the U.S. House of Representatives and Senate would be abolished. "Microsoft isn't a democracy," Gates said, "yet look how well we're doing." When asked about the rumored acquisition of Canada, Gates said only that Microsoft doesn't comment on unannounced products.

Gates said that U.S. citizens can expect lower taxes, increased government services, discounts on all Microsoft products, and the immediate arrest of all executives of Sun Microsystems Inc. and Netscape Communications.

Founded in 1975, Microsoft (NASDAQ "MSFT") is the worldwide leader in software for personal computers and democratic government. The company offers a wide range of products and services for public, business and personal use, each designed to make it easier and more enjoyable for people to take advantage of the full power of personal computing in a mostly free society.

Founded in 1776, the United States of America is the most successful nation in the history of the world, and has been a beacon of democracy and opportunity for more than 200 years. Headquartered in Washington,

BATTLING BIG BLUE

"When I started in computers in the mid-1980s—was it that long ago?—I was told that IBM was not someone with whom you competed; it was the environment in which you competed. That turned out not to be true," said Larry Ellison, chief executive officer of Oracle Software.[55]

Instead, Ellison discovered that it was Microsoft's shadow that loomed large.

~

Microsoft moved to the front of the software pack when it was given the opportunity to write the operating system for the first IBM Personal Computer. But the PC project planted bad feelings that eventually led to a rift between Microsoft and IBM.

In what *Byte* magazine described as either "an incredible act of charity or stupidity," IBM granted Microsoft the right to sell versions of MS-DOS, the operating system that it developed for the PC, to other manufacturers.[56] In fact, Gates allowed IBM to use MS-DOS on the PC at practically no charge, as long as Microsoft could license the system to others. Because the IBM PC was assembled from off-the-shelf parts, replicating the machine was easy. Millions of clones were built by competitors, ranging from large companies to backroom assemblers, and most clones ran MS-DOS, building a powerful revenue base for Microsoft.

∿

IBM employees who worked on the PC project were furious that IBM's market share quickly eroded while Microsoft's share exploded:

"The bitterness was unbelievable," said a former IBM designer. "People were really upset. Gates was raping IBM. It's incomprehensible."[57]

Cultural differences between old-line IBM and upstart Microsoft only made matters worse.

"Microsoft's model is only good people. If you're not good, you don't stick around. IBM's is more a masses-of-asses kind of program," said Ed Iacobucci, once IBM's design manager on the OS/2 project.[58]

∿

In the late 1980s *The Wall Street Journal* printed an apocryphal memo that circulated at IBM regarding a rowing race between Microsoft and IBM. Microsoft won the race, so an IBM task force was named to look into the loss. The committee discovered that on the Microsoft scull, eight people rowed and one steered. On the IBM team, eight steered and one rowed. The

IBM task force recommended that the rower row harder.

～

Gates often says he would have liked to see the relationship between Microsoft and IBM continue, but things finally fell apart in 1989 while the companies were partners on IBM's next generation OS/2 operating system. Gates and IBM engineers differed over how the operating system should be configured. Finally IBM decided it could write the OS/2 operating system itself and essentially kicked Microsoft out of the partnership.

> *"We had to compete against the largest company in the computer industry, which was fighting us with operating system software we had helped develop."*[59]

～

Gates claimed that IBM always had been ambivalent about its relationship with Microsoft, and that unnerved him. Around 1986, in an attempt to mend the relationship between the two companies, Gates offered IBM a 10 percent share of Microsoft. IBM turned the offer down. Silly them. The $100-million investment would have been worth more than $10 billion by 1997.[60]

～

Gates said that one of Microsoft's retreat exercises helped him through the crisis:

" ... during the days of Microsoft's partnership with IBM, one of the small breakout groups would always examine the question: 'How should we prepare ourselves in case our most important partner decides not to work with us anymore?'

"Having gone through that exercise over a period of five years, we were more prepared to cope when IBM pulled out of the partnership in 1992."[61]

~

Author Paul Carroll agreed that IBM waffled on the OS/2 project because it didn't trust Microsoft. IBM should have either cut the project off or joined it wholeheartedly. "Instead, IBM made a halfhearted divorce and offered a halfhearted embrace. IBM wound up with a bad product and an angry partner."[62]

~

Because IBM did not see the importance of graphics and color on the PC screen, the company did nothing to stop Gates from developing Windows. Windows eventually took away the market for which OS/2 was written.

"It took Gates almost nine years to get a good version of Windows on the market," wrote Carroll, "but [IBM executives] were so slow on the uptake that they gave Gates all the time he needed and let him get Windows well entrenched among customers."[63]

~

By 1993 IBM's earnings fell to a minus $7.11 per share, down from $5.26 in 1990. The stock price lost 67 percent of its value, falling to a low of $20.31 from IBM's 1991 high of $61.56. That year Lou Gerstner replaced John Akers as CEO.

Gates's analysis of IBM's situation:

> *"I don't think any company will ever again have the position that IBM had. But Gerstner has the opportunity to unleash a lot of great technologies and the great ideas that are still inside IBM."[64]*

NOTE: After a period of intensely painful restructuring, IBM continues to survive and compete in the computer industry. By 1997 the company earned $6.01 per share and the stock traded as high as $113.50.

～

The work that Microsoft did with IBM changed the computer industry forever:

> *"The most important thing we have done at Microsoft is to create an 'open' operating system platform—first MS-DOS and now Windows—for personal computers. This has allowed tens of thousands of hardware companies and millions of software developers to create products that all work together for the benefit of the consumer. This continuous cycle of innovation has led to PCs that today are more powerful, easier to use, and less expensive than ever before. People sometimes take all this for granted, but if you*

look at how other companies like IBM and Sun have approached computing, you see a big difference in our approach compared to theirs. Their's is a high-cost, low-volume, proprietary approach. Ours is a low-cost, high-volume approach in which any company, including our competitors, can write software and create hardware that works with the open Windows platform."[65]

~

No hard feelings from IBM's former chairman, John Akers, who invited Bill Gates to join the national United Way board just as Gates's mother Mary was ending her tenure on it.[66]

BATTLING FOR THE HECK OF IT

Gates is known for being confrontational, rude, and condescending. According to one report, he simply ignored a flight attendant who asked him to turn off his laptop as a plane was landing. When asked questions that he doesn't like, Gates has cultivated an intimidating glare.

~

Colleagues at Microsoft seem used to Gates's contentiousness. Josh Quittner, a columnist for *Slate*, Microsoft's online magazine, made fun of it in one of his columns. Gates, in the joke, apparently didn't like a piece that was scheduled to run on *Slate*:

"Have it killed," Gates ordered Kinsley. "You mean,

'have him killed,'" Kinsley replied, referring to the author of the *Slate* article. "No, you fools," Gates shrieked. "Kill the piece! Kill the piece!"[67]

~

Gates shouldn't give interviews when he's tired and cranky.

In a legendary 1994 encounter with television reporter Connie Chung, Gates's testiness was captured on tape. Chung wanted to know about a copyright infringement dispute between Microsoft and a smaller company, Stac Electronics. Stac was awarded $120 million by a jury, but the same jury found Stac guilty of appropriating Microsoft's trade secrets and awarded Microsoft $13.7 million.

The ABC *Eye to Eye* segment began with a clip of Gary Clow, chairman of Stac.

Clow: A lot of people make the analogy that competing with Bill Gates is like playing hardball. I'd say it's more like a knife fight.

The camera cut to Gates in his office, where Chung asked for a response to Clow.

Gates: I've never heard any of these things. You're saying, like, knife fight? That's silliness, it's childish. I mean, why be the mouthpiece for that kind of silliness? Why doesn't he just say—anyway—because it has nothing to do with the patent lawsuit, it has to do with just craziness, a sort of David versus Goliath thing out of it.

Gates then turned his back and spoke to someone off camera.

Gates: Well, I'm done.

He then stood up, took off the microphone and ambled out of the office. Chung pursued, asking for one more question, but Gates refused.[68]

NOTE: Microsoft appealed the copyright infringement decision, but before a ruling was received, the companies made an out-of-court settlement involving a cross-license agreement and Microsoft's purchase of a 15 percent stake in Stac.

~

A 1996 interview with *Upside* magazine shows how impatient Gates can become with reporters:

Upside commented that Wall Street analysts were concerned that high-tech companies had fallen short of earnings expectations, Intel in particular.

Gates: Yeah, they only made $800 million.
Upside: But it was less than Intel was expecting, at least in its board business.

Gates: Intel didn't expect to buy so much RAM [random access memory] at an inappropriate price and take a write-off. That they didn't expect. That cost them 5 cents a share. They were only up 40 percent year-to-year!

Upside then asked if a slowdown could be expected in the industry.

Gates: Name an industry that's going to grow faster than the PC industry. I mean . . . Now don't start crying. It's very sad. This is sad news. This is going to be tough for you. We might only grow at 18 percent. Now that's on top of 60 million units a year. This has got to be rough, very rough.[69]

～

Stuart Alsop, a newsletter publisher, once claimed that Gates was obfuscating issues on Microsoft's object linking and embedding (OLE) project because he didn't yet know how the technology would work. After the column was printed Alsop says Gates accosted him at a trade meeting, assaulting him at length with colorful language.

Alsop wasn't surprised, " . . . I'm kind of grinning and thinking, 'hoo boy, did I hit a soft spot.'"[70]

～

But in the dark wire tunnels of the electronic empire, every misdeed seems to get avenged, even if the avenger was not the person harmed. It's some sort of law of cosmic return. On the eve of Gates's appearance before a U.S. Senate panel to defend Microsoft's business practices, a hacker shut down computers coast to coast that were running on Microsoft's NT software. The shutdown appeared to be merely an irritating prank, and apparently no data were lost or stolen. Microsoft urged its customers to download a "patch" to protect its machines from future high jinx.[71]

MICROSOFT
MISTAKES

EXPECT FAILURE

Gates once kept a memo to himself entitled, "Microsoft's Greatest Mistakes." Number one on the list was letting Novell, a competitor, capture the computer networking market.[1] But Gates more recently has said the company's late awakening to the growth and development of the Internet was its greatest error.

Yet Microsoft is persistent, and often that persistence pays off. Twice it failed in an attempt to enter the market for small, hand-held computers, but in 1998 it was back in the market with a third attempt, the palm-size PC.

~

In 1993 Microsoft tried to buy America Online, the electronic service, for an estimated $268 million, but was rebuffed. When Microsoft decided to start its own on-line network, an AOL executive predicted that interactive services would become Microsoft's Vietnam.

Microsoft Network was launched in mid-1995 in

50 countries and 26 languages. The service was not particularly reliable, its billing service was messed up, and consumers did not flock to it. Although even its own management admits that MSN always might lag behind competitors, Microsoft continued to improve the on-line connection service. A Microsoft spokesperson said that MSN may turn a profit in 1998.

~

Gates was a keynote speaker at the 1998 Consumer Electronics Show in Las Vegas, where a dazzling array of gadgets, appliances, and toys were displayed.

> *"Now, I think it's valuable to remember that not all the great new products here go on to be a success. I know many years ago, John Sculley came and talked about digital convergence, a trillion-dollar market, and introduced Newton. That product proved to be a little bit ahead of its time, [which] was probably tough on his career. Four years ago, I came and introduced a product called Microsoft Bob. Now, Microsoft Bob sold even less than the Newton. And so, I must have a more forgiving board of directors than John Sculley had, because here I am trying again with some great new products."[2]*

NOTE: For more about Microsoft Bob, an easy-to-use home computer interface released by Microsoft in 1995, turn to "MISS."

~

Gates says Microsoft will continue to have failures, some of them visible to the public, others not so visible:

> *"But we can afford to make a few mistakes now, and we can't afford not to try. Because of the scope of opportunity, and with shareholders' expectations for us to keep sales and profits growing, everything's about big horizons at Microsoft now. But, hey, we can tackle big horizons. We're expected to tackle big horizons. We love big horizons."[3]*

THE TROUBLE WITH DEADLINES

Microsoft has a checkered past with deadlines.

The first Windows operating system was delivered in 1985, two years after it was promised, and even then the program fell short of expectations. Windows NT was scheduled for delivery March 30, 1991; it was released July 26, 1993. A later-generation Windows was announced for 1993 but became Windows 95.

Despite the slipped deadlines critics claim Microsoft often releases substandard products just to get to market before competitors. But eventually, as upgrades come along, these products function as ground-breaking software.

Gates says that delays are inevitable because of the nature of the work. The original Windows 95 packs 8.5 million of lines of code, which expands to 14 million lines when upgraded with Internet Explorer. Microsoft has added about half a million lines a year to its operating system since it released the first DOS in 1981.[4] The programs take months of testing, both inside the company and outside in beta, or customer, tests.

"If you take quality as a given, you are always going to have some uncertainty in the date."[5]

～

"Every product is like that. If you're confused about that, then it's a good time for me to straighten that out—the date is not the fixed thing for any of these products. Period. It's not. And everyone else, I think, knows that."[6]

～

On February 10, 1998, Microsoft ran a glitzy full-page ad in *The Wall Street Journal* aimed at the small business owner. It promised "We'll send you our small business information packet when you call 1-800-60source. It's full of relevant, pertinent advice to help you succeed." The 800 number operator explained that the packets weren't ready yet but would ship around the first of March. The packet did not arrive until the end of July, 1998, though Microsoft denies that this was vaporware.

～

A Microsoft employee explained that the company was good at programming but bad at scheduling.

～

MISS

Originally, Microsoft targeted main market power users, sophisticated professional or semiprofessional computer operators. In the 1990s, however, Microsoft realized that there was a massive market among those who merely utilize computers as a means to some end. These computer users are like drivers who use their automobiles to get around but do not know or care how a car works. They just need simple, reliable equipment.

"Of all the big initiatives at Microsoft, simplicity is No. 1."[7]

～

At the 1998 Consumer Electronics Show in Las Vegas, to demonstrate how unnecessarily complex software has become, Gates showed how difficult it is to find the author's credits for Microsoft Excel 95, which are hidden in an "Easter egg." First, select row 95 in a new workbook, press the tab key, choose the help menu's "About Microsoft Excel" command, hold down the shift, ctrl, and alt keys at the same time while clicking the tech support button.

"This puts you in a roomlike environment that you navigate with the four arrow keys. Go up a stairway to see scrolling lists of credits. Turn away from the stairway and type 'excelkfa' to reveal a zigzag walkway that leads to photographs of some of the people who created the software. It's hard to navigate the walkway without falling off—so beware!"[8]

NOTE: Gates intended this example to be humorous. Programmers have some fun hiding their by-lines in Easter eggs.

～

It may be too late for computer programmers to follow the KISS principle—keep it simple stupid. They have to go back and MISS—make it simple stupid. Gates says Web browsers in particular must be self-explanatory:

> "There's no way users are going to learn all these protocols and acronyms, and we have to hide that from them. We have to hide the idea of even installing software. They have to think of it as all browsing, even though behind the scenes there's code moving down to the local machine and being verified."[9]

～

> "Today's quest is for simplicity, which will lead to sharply lower total costs of owning and operating information technology. The debate is over which simplification strategy is best."[10]

～

> "If you could basically talk to your computer and say the information you wanted and it understood where to go get it, that would be a lot simpler than clicking around like a madman."[11]

～

"And so, if you ask a question like, what is the fastest computer chip available, you won't read about potato chips being delivered in fast trucks or something, because the semantics will be understood."[12]

~

One of Microsoft's first products designed to help novice computer users flopped:

"Our failures tend to result from markets being too small. Microsoft Bob was a product a couple of years ago that used on-screen cartoon characters to carry out tasks for people. Unfortunately, the software demanded more performance than typical computer hardware could deliver at the time and there wasn't an adequately large market. Bob died."[13]

Some consumers thought Microsoft Bob was too simpleminded, and that once people had used the program a few times, they felt beyond it. Apparently, the project manager for Microsoft Bob was forgiven, since Melinda French Gates is still married to the boss.

PLAYING CATCH-UP ON THE INTERNET

The speed of the Internet revolution surprised even future-thinking Bill Gates. He knew that the great electronic playground created by the government for academics and scientists was growing in popularity during his April 1993 retreat at Hood Canal. But at the time consumers did not seem drawn to the 11-

year-old Internet. By the next October, just six months later, things were moving.

"As it happened, the lightning struck early. The public got a taste of interactivity on the Internet's World Wide Web and said, 'We're not waiting for a better solution! Let's go!'"[14]

~

"The closest thing to it I can think of is the Gold Rush where everybody went off to find their fortune. And people were fairly surprised at how it all turned out. It [the gold rush] did a great job of developing the economy in California, and it was really the people providing the infrastructure who were the most successful."[15]

~

Business Week reported that after Gates realized what had happened, "Microsoft launched postmortems over what should have been and what could be the next time. This process helped save the company. In 1994, at an executive retreat, younger employees boldly spoke out about Microsoft's failure to deal with the Net—and implicitly, Gates's failure to lead them into this new territory. Gates did a 180."[16]

"Some people draw an analogy to IBM missing out on really benefitting from PCs—this [Microsoft's miscue on the Internet] is not the same. We are focused on this. It doesn't guarantee us anything because in high tech no one has a guaranteed posi-

tion. The question is, will Microsoft execute well on pulling all these pieces together?"[17]

~

Within 45 days Microsoft had a new product and a pricing strategy for the Internet.

"It came to a fever pitch and was recognized as a crisis. It wouldn't have happened if we had a tired nervous system."[18]

~

"It was a wonderful chance for me to go to the company and remind them, 'Hey, we don't have a guaranteed place. We've got to take this Internet initiative and really surprise the world with what we can do.'"[19]

Shock might have been the more appropriate description of the world's reaction. See "Battling the Competition" and "Battling the Government."

ATTACK THE FUTURE

THINK WEEK

Gates knows that time pressures prevent him from contemplating matters in depth and putting them in perspective. That's why he schedules time away from his office.

> *"A couple of times a year I go away for a think week, during which I read books and other materials my colleagues believe I should see to stay up-to-date. These materials often include Ph.D. theses exploring the frontiers of computer science."[1]*

Gates usually spends his think weeks at Gateaway, a retreat on Washington's Hood Canal, where he first started vacationing with his family as a child. Hood Canal is 90 minutes by car from Seattle. Gates bought the three and a half acres of waterfront property for about $650,000. He added a tennis court, spa, and four north-western-style cottages, which his father and sisters use. Gates's own villa doubles as a corporate retreat center.

WE SET THE STANDARDS

In the beginning of any new industry, whether it is automobiles, airplanes, VCRs, wireless communications, or computers, there is a battle for industry standards—to get everyone to do things the same way. For example, it finally became standard in the United States to drive on the right side of the road and put steering wheels on the left side of the car. Bill Gates and Paul Allen captured enormous market share early in their careers by writing the version of the BASIC language that became standard for the microcomputer. Next, MS-DOS became the standard operating system for PCs, which eventually was replaced by several generations of Windows.

Setting the standards became a Microsoft priority.

∼

Gates was accused of damaging Apple Computer by mimicking its graphical interface when Microsoft created Windows. At first, however, Gates wanted to work with Apple in creating a standard graphical interface operating system for PCs. In July 1985 Bill Gates wrote a memo to John Sculley, then head of Apple:

> *"Apple must make Macintosh a standard. But no personal computer company, not even IBM, can create a standard without independent support."*

Gates suggested that Apple license its technology, including Mac-compatible units, to others and offered a list of 20 companies worldwide that Apple should work with.

> *"Microsoft is very willing to help Apple implement this strategy. We are familiar with the key manufacturers, their strategies and strengths. We also have a great deal of experience in OEMing [porting between makes] systems software."*[2]

Sculley rejected Gates's offer, thus condemning Apple to a lesser market role. Apple sued Microsoft for taking the "look and feel" of its system, but lost.

~

Java, the "write once—use anywhere" programming language, demonstrates the difficulty in achieving standards in a rapidly evolving, highly competitive industry. Java was introduced by Sun Microsystems in 1995 and has gained a wide following among software developers. But clients complain that Sun is too restrictive in allowing modifications to Java that programmers need. Sun sued both Microsoft and Hewlett-Packard for producing variations. H-P said it decided to act independently out of frustration over "excessive licensing fees" for a consumer-electronics version of Java. These different strains of Java will create the sort of rival-product camps and software incompatibilities that the language was created to avoid.[3]

Microsoft asked Sun to submit its Java programming language to an industry standards body, claiming that a product cannot be both proprietary and have the imprimatur of a standards body.

"Having Microsoft give us advice on open standards is like W.C. Fields giving moral advice to the Mormon Tabernacle Choir," shot back Scott McNealy, Sun's chief executive.[4]

～

Gates insisted that Sun Microsystems wasn't playing fair:

" . . . when Sun went and wrote a Windows clone, which was called WABI, they didn't have any license from us. They're welcome. Go ahead, do that. But when we did Java, we went to them, we signed a license; we paid a fee there. Because we thought, hey, if Java's got a role here, that's valuable. It is sort of illustrative of the contradiction of calling something an open standard when there's one company that controls the trademark and defines what it is. And we have no problem whether it's a standard or not a standard. We think there's some real value there. But we believe that things that are standard should be neutrally managed and things that are a company's products where that company is going to take the risks and get rewards, they should be clearly labeled that way."[5]

～

By the late 1990s, scalability became an important issue. Scalability is a concept that allows standard software to be applied up and down to both sophisticated and simple computers.

"This is the idea of taking PC technology, which, historically, people thought of as low-cost but low-power computing, and moving that up to take on the most difficult software applications, including even applications that historically would have required very expensive mainframes or other large computers."[6]

~

The Micro-jokesters worry that once the standard belongs to Microsoft, the rest of us will be in the dark:

Question: How many Microsoft programmers does it take to change a light bulb?
Answer: None—the company just changes the standard to darkness.[7]

CONNECTIVITY

The standards war is far from over. With more computer users communicating across the Internet, it is imperative that different programs speak a standard, common language. As explained in this 1997 IBM advertisement in a *Wall Street Journal* advertisement entitled "Hava Java": "Perhaps the most profound change that the Web has brought to the IT (information technology) world is a culture of standards. It's this capability that permits universal connectivity and has allowed 80-million-plus people to access the Web."[8]

～

Several companies, including Microsoft, are trying to combine Internet browsing with the home television set. This form of Internet connectivity would be easy and fun for those who don't do word processing, numbers crunching, or other tasks on home computers but would like to use e-mail, surf the Web, or interact with scheduled television programs:

> *"The device we're talking about here has all the benefits of a TV. It's fairly inexpensive; you can stick it in your living room and use a little remote control to control it. But inside are chips that are even more powerful than today's PCs. And if you add a keyboard or printer you can do PC-like things. So it's a device that needs a new name."*[9]

Finally, the industry settled on a simple name for interactive television—the set-top box.

> *"Clearly, we think the path here is to give customers compatibility with what they've learned, what they've invested in, and yet do that with great simplicity."*[10]

～

Microsoft is competing with its old nemeses, Sun and Oracle, in this arena. As usual, the companies have different philosophies on how things will work:

"Microsoft wants to own everything, from soup to nuts, plus content," insists Farid Dibachi, general manager of consumer technologies for Sun Microsystems. "The big difference between us and them is that we provide enabling technologies. At the end of the day, there is going to be a clash between the brand name of Microsoft and the brand names of big consumer-electronics companies."[11]

THINKING ABOUT SOMEDAY

These are exciting times, according to Gates:

> *"We [in the computer industry] have a tremendous opportunity to enhance the ways we think and learn by talking advantage of technology."[12]*

When Gates daydreams about the future, Moore's Law tells him there will be dramatic advances in what computers do and how they do it.

Moore's Law holds that the computing capacity of a microprocessor doubles every year. Gordon Moore, one of the founders of Intel, says that the law came about when in 1965 he was asked to predict the future of semiconductor components for the next ten years. "We'd been about doubling every year since the first planar transistor—I call that Year Zero, 1959—with 1 transistor. We'd gotten up to 64 in six years—in 1965—so I said, 'Aha, it's been doubling every year.' I just said, 'Okay, it's going to continue to do that for ten years.' So I extrapolated a factor of a thousandfold increase in the complexity of circuits, not expecting any real accuracy but wanting to get this idea of the way the components were going to be used. For that ten years, we followed that doubling every year really quite precisely."[13]

At a 1998 conference Gates said he expected Moore's Law to apply for at least 20 more years, even though it will become more difficult to expand technology at past rates.[14]

"Computing will be ubiquitous. You'll have the pocket device and the wall-size device, and (depending on how you set things up) you'll be able to talk to the computer when you're not really paying attention to it. So the term PC will call up a different image than it does now. But what you thought of 15 years ago when you said the term PC and what you think of now are vastly different."[15]

∼

We've long awaited the paperless society. Gates promises us that it's still coming, though he admits that paper won't disappear entirely:

"Handwritten notes will be delivered by mail, and their rarity will give them even more meaning. But eventually there won't be many other kinds of paper trucked around."[16]

Post offices everywhere are scurrying to adapt to the change:

"The Irish Post Office uses PC-based kiosks to accept utility payments, sell lottery tickets, issue passports and licenses for things such as vehicles and to disburse entitlement benefits such as unemployment,

pensions, and child support. The computer system also supports deposits, withdrawals, interest posting and electronic funds transfers."[17]

~

If Gates has his wish, computers will change telephone practices. He got so many unwanted sales and other calls at all hours that he got an unlisted telephone number. Gates must change his telephone number periodically because someone invariably finds the number, then pesters him endlessly. Charging those who make the call would change all of that:

> *"You might say that anybody can ring your phone during the day for a dollar, but that after 5 P.M. it's $5 and after midnight it's $25. Or that after your usual bedtime no one can reach you at any price except a few friends and agencies such as the police. You'll probably charge less to let people leave you voice or e-mail messages—or maybe you won't charge at all. The point is that you, rather than your callers or correspondents, will be in control."*[18]

Apparently, Gates's family and old college buddies have nothing to worry about:

> *"Of course, you can always decide not to charge a person after all, if you're glad you got their message."*[19]

~

Gates says the mixing of video, computer, and on-line technology is a challenge to companies like Microsoft:

"You try to ride the incredible wave that's coming."[20]

⌣

Since the mid-1980s Gates has predicted that we'd soon be chatting away to our computers and that they would talk back.

"Why can't they listen to you when you speak? Why can't they recognize you? If you have a camera on your computer, why doesn't it know who you are when you sit down and then customize itself according to the things it has seen that you like?"[21]

⌣

"As you walk in front of your computer, you have a little camera which will be quite inexpensive. Office [a Microsoft program] will notice who's there and immediately bring up the things that you're interested in on that machine."[22]

⌣

"The future of computing is the computer that talks, listens, sees, and learns."[23]

⌣

"Within a few years, even small, affordable personal computers may have personalities and possibly idiosyncrasies. These machines will speak rather naturally in a human voice, if that's what we want. They will behave as if they understand many of the verbal commands we give. They will try to be helpful. They may even act sympathetic when we face frustrations. Giving computers the trappings of intelligence will

make them easier to use. But it won't mean they really think—yet."[24]

~

"In ten years [from 1997] there will be better input systems—handwriting, speech, visual recognition . . . As much as 90 percent of the operating system code will go to these new capabilities."[25]

~

When computers get that smart, you'll need a supervising computer:

"Imagine a single wallet-size device from which you could activate all of your other devices—your table-size or desktop personal computer, appliances in your house, whatever large screen display you have in your home. I envision a wallet PC that allows interchange and communication between all these other devices."[26]

~

Chatter boxes may be near, but mind-reading computers will take awhile:

"It will take much longer before we can hook computers directly to our central nervous systems, so that images in our heads are expressed directly to a screen."[27]

Gates recalled that when he was a kid, it was fun to look at the card stuck in the library books and see who had read them before you. An invasion of privacy perhaps, but nothing compared to what's ahead:

"As people really wake up to how much information about them is stored on computers and how it can be used, the issue of privacy—the balancing of individual liberties against the public's right to know—will be a hot topic."[28]

Nothing demonstrates the impact that computers and the Internet will have on society better than the problems faced by Microsoft when writing its Encarta CD-ROM encyclopedia. Was the American Thomas Edison or the British inventor Sir Thomas Swan responsible for the incandescent light bulb? Did Alexander Graham Bell or the Italian-American Antonio Meucci invent the telephone? You'd better say Swan in the British version and Meucci in the Italian one, though it's okay to explain that shortly after, and working independently, Edison and Bell came up with the most commercially popular versions of these life-changing inventions.

In the British version of Encarta, a small group of islands off the coast of Argentina are called the Falklands; in the Spanish version, they are called the Islas Malvinas. In the Japanese version, the discussion of cherries and cherry blossoms contains ten photographs and six pages of text, while in the U.S. Encarta there are only two pictures and five paragraphs.

In the Korean edition, Microsoft made the mistake of saying that a small state in southern Korea, known as Kaya to the Koreans and Mimana to the Japanese, had been "dominated" by Japan in the third and fourth centuries.

> *"Before we corrected it, this error provoked outrage in South Korea, where one major newspaper called for a boycott of all Microsoft products."[29]*

Microsoft plans an international edition of Encarta to be accessible on-line. Gates realizes that Microsoft's policy of "local, educated reality," or opening eyes in different regions of the world to different perspectives on history, geography, religion, and the like, may be unpopular.

> *"In the long run, exposing people to worldwide perspectives should be healthy. Americans can benefit from a better understanding of the Asian or European view of important cultural and scientific events, and vice versa."[30]*

~

Before anything changes, Gates says people have to want the change:

> *" . . . technological advances alone aren't enough to drive social change. At least some people have to embrace change or it won't happen."[31]*

OTHERS SAY

BILLOPHOBIA

Gates has been called a swashbuckler of the Information Age, a highwayman of the infobahn, or an *enfant terrible*. He has made plenty of enemies during his remarkable life journey. Gates tends to dazzle people with his intellect but not his personality.

~

Some software makers say they are afraid to meet with Microsoft to discuss potential joint partnerships. They accuse Microsoft of "date rape." That is, Microsoft requests meetings to discuss mutual projects; examines the potential partners, products, innovations, techniques, or marketing plans; then appropriates whatever it likes.

Daniel Bricklin, chief technology officer at Trellix Corp. says working with Microsoft is like dancing with an elephant: "It's very scary to be dancing with an elephant. They look at what you're doing and borrow whatever they can, and that hasn't changed since I first started working with them."[1]

PC World columnist Steve Bass summed up public sentiment in a 1997 column:

"Everyone picks on the software giant. Well, back up the dump truck, folks, it's an easy target. It wasn't always that way. Microsoft—and Uncle Bill—used to be my heroes. I admired their entrepreneurial, guerrilla-marketing style; I even emulated them in my seminar business. But the company has grown arrogant and overbearing, with a cavalier attitude toward its bugs (a verboten word in Redmond) and a take-no-prisoners approach toward its competitors. (There, I've said it. Lightning didn't strike and I feel lots better.)"[2]

~

One of Gates's most vituperative critics is Robert X. Cringley, the pseudonym of an *Infoworld* magazine columnist and author of *Accidental Empires*:

"My secret suspicion," wrote Cringley, "is that Microsoft's cult of personality hides a deep-down fear on Gates's part that maybe he doesn't really know it all. A few times I've seen him cornered by some techie who is not from Microsoft and not in awe, a techie who knows more about the subject at hand than Bill Gates ever will. I've seen a flash of fear in Gates's eyes then. Even with you or me, topics can range beyond Bill's grasp, and that's when he uses his 'I don't know how technical you are' line."[3]

Cringley conceded, however, that in the 1979 premier issue of *InfoWorld*, there were 19 advertisers, of which only two remained in business by 1992. One was Microsoft and the other was a Palo Alto computer repairman who operated out of a storefront.[4]

~

Steven Jobs, cofounder of Apple Computer, has sympathy (of a sort) for Gates:

"I wish him the best, I really do. I just think he and Microsoft are a bit narrow. He'd be a broader guy if he had dropped acid once or gone off to an ashram when he was younger."[5]

~

Esther Dyson, the PC guru, suggests that many of Bill Gates's critics suffer from Bill envy. "Just about all the guys in the industry have it. It makes them feel inadequate and it makes them do stupid things. He's the Rorschach blot of the industry. What people think of Bill tells more about them that it does about him."[6]

~

Forbes magazine prefers the word "Billophobia" to Bill envy, "since it goes beyond envy and embraces fear and dislike."[7]

~

Even those who have complained publicly about Microsoft have mixed emotions:

"His image as a nerd and a visionary hacker is baloney—Gates is one helluva sharp businessman and a top-notch negotiator. Just look at how he worked out a deal that had Microsoft working with IBM to develop an operating system that Microsoft then turned around and sold to IBM's competitors. I can't believe it. Gates is a phenomenon," said Phillipe Kahn, president of Borland International.[8]

~

Mitch Kapor, founder of Lotus, says, "Microsoft represents the best of ourselves or the worst."[9]

FRIENDS SAY

Getting a fix on the real Bill Gates is not easy, largely because there are so few people like him in the world. Is Gates dishonest and deceitful, or as Gay Kawasaki, formerly of Apple Computers, believes, just incredibly tough?[10] He has as many friends as he does foes.

Mike Maples, a Microsoft executive vice president:

"Bill is just smarter than everyone else. There are probably more smart people per square foot right here than anywhere else in the world, but Bill is just smarter."[11]

~

Alan Kerr, senior VP executive group director for Ogilvy & Mather, which formerly was Microsoft's advertising agency: "Everybody is waiting for this guy to slip. He hasn't slipped, and there's very little chance that he will. Everything that he keeps his hands in will work, and he will win. He's that good, he's that smart."[12]

～

Rich Karlgaard, publisher of *Forbes* magazine: "Mr. Gates has earned his success. He has always paid himself a low salary, preferring to bet on the rise of his stock. In other words, he has allied his own pocketbook with those of his employees and shareholders. He has not squandered money on unworthy charities, despite enormous public pressure. Until he got married in 1994, Mr. Gates toiled most nights in his office until 10 o'clock."[13]

～

Computer industry pioneer Ken Olsen: "When someone is as successful as Gates is, there is a tendency for just anybody to be jealous, and that should not be a factor [in determining whether Microsoft broke antitrust laws]. They are tough competitors, but they do have a level of integrity."[14]

Gordon Eubanks, chairman of the Cupertino, California-based software company, Symantec: "I don't think they have done things we wouldn't do ourselves, or that people who have complained the most wouldn't do either."[15]

～

InfoWorld columnist Bob Lewis took flak for calling Gates a revolutionary. Some readers just didn't like

Gates. Others said Gates couldn't be a revolutionary because the ideas he popularized were not his own:

"True enough," wrote Lewis. "Bill Gates has spent his career recognizing good ideas, turning them into products, and marketing them successfully. Successful political revolutionaries have similar histories. Washington led the army; John Locke theorized about democracy before him. Lenin, Mao Tse-tung, and Castro led successful revolutions; Karl Marx theorized about communism before they used his theories to justify their revolutions. Revolutionaries aren't investors. They are not theoreticians. They're not pioneers. Those are other people, important people. They just aren't revolutionaries."[16]

~

PC Computing columnist Paul Somerson notes that computer users blame Microsoft for their troubles because it's easy:

" . . . when all else fails, blame Microsoft. It's easy to pigeonhole them as annoyingly smug young millionaires, a stereotype fostered by competitors who secretly wish they had pulled off what Bill Gates did, and by creepy headline-hoggers like Assistant U.S. Attorney General Joel Klein and Netscape lawyer Gary Reback, who would love to see Microsoft destroyed. This somehow would be good for the economy. Yeah, right. It's just what Mark Twain supposedly wrote: Sacred cows make the best hamburgers."[17]

~

Sheldon Adelson, CEO of the company that organizes the massive computer trade show Comdex, says Gates makes a large target: "He's bigger than Sinatra. He comes out and says 'I did it my way,' and obviously no one can argue."[18]

BUFFETT AND BILL

If there is rivalry between Bill Gates and super-investor Warren Buffett, it is a friendly one. The two billionaires were introduced in 1991 when Buffett visited Meg Greenfield, editorial page editor of the *Washington Post*, and a friend of Gates's mother. Mary Gates invited Greenfield and her guests to the Gates's Hood Canal retreat on July 5.

Greenfield described the day: "We all stuffed ourselves into my ancient Subaru and drove out to spend the day." Gates and his wife-to-be Melinda arrived by helicopter.

"I was not unaware that this was an interesting pairing. Bill and Warren began a very intense conversation, and it went from there," Greenfield said.[19]

In addition to their billions of dollars and despite the difference in their ages, Buffett and Gates have much in common. They like each other's jokes, food choices (heavy on the hamburgers), and philosophy of life. Both consider themselves mostly Democrat, though their fathers were Republicans. Both love their work.

Gates was surprised that he and Buffett, chairman and majority shareholder of Berkshire Hathaway, Inc., hit it off so easily:

"Whenever somebody says to me, 'You've got to meet my friend so-and-so; he's the smartest guy ever,' my defenses go up. Most people are quick to conclude that someone or something they encounter personally is exceptional. This is just human nature. Everybody wants to know someone or something superlative. As a result, people overestimate the merit of that to which they've been exposed. So the fact that people called Warren Buffett unique didn't impress me much."[20]

～

Buffett once challenged Gates to a game of dice, using a set of four unusual dice with a combination of numbers from 0 to 12 on the sides. Buffett suggested that each of them choose one of the dice, then discard the other two. They would bet on who would roll the highest number most often. Buffett offered to let Gates pick his die first. This suggestion instantly aroused Gates's curiosity. He asked to examine the dice, after which he demanded that Buffett choose first.

"It wasn't immediately evident that because of the clever selection of numbers for the dice they were nontransitive," Gates said. "The mathematical principle of transitivity, that if A beats B and B beats C, then A beats C, did not apply. Assuming ties were rerolled, each of the four dice could be beaten by one of the others: Die A would beat B an average of 11 out of 17 rolls—almost two-thirds of the time. Die B would beat C with the same frequency. Likewise, C would beat D 11/17 of the time too. And improbable as it sounds, die D would beat A just as often."[21]

⌣

Gates and Buffett agree that they were lucky to be born in the right time and place.

"Warren says if he'd been born a few thousand years ago, he'd probably have been some animal's lunch. But he was born into an age that has a stock market and rewards Warren for his unique understanding of the market."[22]

⌣

On a three-week jaunt through China, Gates and Buffett played bridge, visited the Great Wall, flew kites, and ate at McDonald's, using discount coupons that Buffett had brought along.

At the Forbidden City, where they were shown huge ancient scrolls that were rolled and unrolled by women trained for the task, Gates whispered to Buffett, "There's a $2 fine if you return a scroll unwound."[23]

⌣

A video made for the 1996 Berkshire Hathaway annual meeting showed Gates stuffing coins into a pay telephone in China, calling his wife back in Seattle, trying to explain how he'd lost the number-one spot on the "richest list" to Buffett. Melinda did not take kindly to the loss. "But honey!!!" wailed Gates.[24]

~

Buffett urged Gates to read *The Intelligent Investor*, the 1949 classic written by Benjamin Graham, one of Buffett's Columbia professors. Gates has been impressed by Buffett's analysis of business fundamentals and his long-term perspective:

> *"I think Warren has had more effect on the way I think about my business and the way I think about running it than any business leader."*[25]

~

Buffett also influenced the Gates family in other ways.

"Population [control] has always been more my game than Trey's," explained Bill Gates, Sr. "I didn't know Trey had any feelings about the issue until several years ago when we were sitting around talking to Warren and Susie Buffett in Palm Springs. I told him then that we should be productive and start generating some requests (for grants). On our trip to China with the Buffetts in 1995, we all made a point of visiting a family-planning center at a small village on the Yangtze River."[26]

~

Although Buffett and Gates have much in common, there are important differences. Buffett avoids technology stocks because he doesn't understand the underlying business:

> *"Unfortunately for Warren, the world of technology knows no boundaries. Over time, most business assets will be affected by technology's broad reach—although Gillette, Coca-Cola, and See's [candy] should be safe."*[27]

These three companies are among Berkshire Hathaway's core holdings.

～

Buffett says this about Gates:

"I'm not competent to judge his technical ability, but I regard his business savvy as extraordinary. If Bill had started a hot dog stand, he would have become the hot dog king of the world."[28]

～

Gates took up bridge—a game his father loves—after meeting Buffett. Gates and Buffett study with the same bridge coach, Sharon Osberg of San Francisco. Gates can relate to Osberg, who during the day is a computer systems analyst. Both Buffett and Gates subscribe to the same Internet bridge club, Okbridge. Anyone can join by downloading Okbridge at www.okbridge.com. There is a $99 annual membership fee.

~

Gates says that playing bridge on-line changed Buffett's attitude about computers:

> *"For the first six months he would come home and play for hours on end. Despite the fact that he had studiously stayed away from technology and technology investing, once he tried the computer, he was hooked. Now, many weeks Warren uses on-line services more than I do."*[29]

~

Buffett and Gates played a round of golf in the summer of 1997 at the Omaha Country Club. "We had a small wager," said Buffett, "but the outcome did not affect the *Forbes* [richest] rankings."[30]

LIVING AT THE PINNACLE

THE WORLD OF THE CYBERRICH

In 1997 Gates's wealth was estimated at $35 billion, making him the richest American ever. In 1998, that jumped 40 percent to $51 billion. But wealth is relative. In *The Wealthy 100: From Benjamin Franklin to Bill Gates—a Ranking of the Richest Americans, Past and Present*, Gates is listed as thirty-first. The book ranks the top 100 wealthiest Americans by the ratio of their wealth to the gross national product. John D. Rockefeller, who was first on the list, controlled 1/65th of the nation's wealth during his lifetime. In 1995 Gates only controlled 1/425th of the U.S. GNP.

But he is rich enough. Between June 1996 and June 1997, Gates's stake in Microsoft jumped from $17 billion to $35 billion. "The [additional] $18 billion works out to $49.5 million a day, seven days a week, or $2.1 million per hour, 24 hours a day, $35,000 per minute, or $583 a second," calculates *Fortune* magazine. "These are terms that anyone will recognize as a mite larger than the numbers on one's own pay stub."[1]

~

Some Internetters struggle to grasp the enormity of Gates's wealth:

"If you presume that he has worked 14 hours a day on every business day of the year since [founding Microsoft in 1975] that means he's been making money at a staggering half-million dollars per hour, around $150 per second. Which means that if, on his way into the office, should he see or drop a $500 bill on the ground, it's just not worth his time to bend over and pick it up. He would make more just heading off to work."[2]

If you push the calculations forward to figure in the accelerating rate at which Gates's fortune is piling up, the picture gets even loonier. Soon he'll just have to leave $1,000 bills laying on the ground, if ever he were to spot such a rare, uncirculated item.

~

Stories like the life of Bill Gates keep people motivated:

"It is still possible to be a Vanderbilt, an Astor, a Rockefeller," says media mogul David Geffen. "You can still do that, you can be Bill Gates, you can be Rupert Murdoch."[3]

~

In 1994, with a net worth of $9.35 billion, Bill Gates, 38, shoved Warren Buffett, 64, from the head of the list of wealthiest Americans. But Buffett had a scheme. For years he kept a dart board in his outer office, which he claimed was his stock picker. Buffett said he'd now lost faith in the board.

"It doesn't work anymore, so I'm going to give it to Bill Gates," Buffett said. "I'll let him keep the dart board so that we can keep him in second place."[4]

That worked for a while and Buffett regained the lead, but by 1997 Gates seemed to be racing out ahead. Both men treat the richest status as a non-issue joke. Buffett lives modestly and doesn't cash many of his shares. Gates spends more of his money but still calls the list "silly."

"If I had some set idea of a finish line, don't you think I would have crossed it years ago?"[5]

~

Both Buffett and Gates have made thousands of other people wealthy. In 1997 Microsoft cofounder Paul Allen was the fifth richest person in the world, with $14.1 billion. (The *Forbes* list excludes royal families.) Microsoft employees also are well rewarded, thanks to their stock options. By 1993, just seven years after its initial public offering, a $2,000 investment in Microsoft would have been worth $70,000.

~

The first billion comes the hardest. After that, money pours in from everywhere. For *The Road Ahead*, a book on which Gates collaborated with Nathan Myhrvold and journalist Peter Rinearson, Penguin paid a $2.5

million advance. The book has sold well, partly because it is often hawked at events where Gates speaks. Royalties from the book are donated to charity.

～

Despite his wealth and power, Gates is not the highest paid executive in the United States or even the highest paid at Microsoft. Chief operating officer Robert Herbold earns the most, bringing in $1.2 million in annual salary and bonuses, while Bernard Vergnes, president of Microsoft Europe, collects $714,000. Gates pulls down around $525,000 in salary and bonuses. Maybe he'll have to ask himself for a raise, though, since the King County tax assessor has demanded around $580,000 in 1998 taxes on the Gates's new home.

NOTE: For more details on Gates's real estate, see "The Lake Washington Estates."

～

Gates claims not to be motivated by money:

> *"Even today, what interests me isn't making money per se. If I had to choose between my job and having great wealth, I'd choose the job. It's a much bigger thrill to lead a team of thousands of talented, bright people than it is to have a big bank account."[6]*

～

> *"Business is a good game. Lots of competition and a minimum of rules. You keep score with money."[7]*

~

Gates says he doesn't keep track of his net worth:

"I'm pretty good at multiplication, but I never look at the stock price so I don't know what number to multiply by."[8]

~

Keith Herrmann, an autograph collector from North Carolina, specializes in the John Henrys of CEOs. Herrmann sent letters to the *Fortune* 500 CEOs requesting a signed photograph. About 200 accommodated, including Bill Gates. Herrmann was excited about Gates's response, until a few weeks later he got a duplicate photo and signature. He then suspected that he was getting an autograph signed by an autopen, which Gates is rumored to use to sign his correspondence. Big disappointment for Herrmann. A genuine signature of the world's wealthiest man is worth about $35. An autopen version is worth zip.[9]

~

Wealthy people get invited to nice places:

When *Time* magazine celebrated its seventy-fifth birthday, luminaries of all sorts were invited, including, among many others, President Clinton, Joe DiMaggio, Lauren Bacall, and Muhammad Ali. Gates was asked to deliver a toast to the Wright Brothers.

~

On the other hand, wealthy people get some very nasty mail.

"Recalling Willie Sutton, we ask: Why do you try to rob Bill Gates? A: Because that's where the money is."[10]

Amusing observation, but one threat to Gates, his wife Melinda, their toddler daughter, Jennifer Katharine, and Microsoft executive Steve Ballmer was truly frightening:

> On or about March 14, 1997, within the Western District of Washington, Adam Quinn Pletcher knowingly, and with intent to extort a sum of money from William H. Gates III, did cause to be sent and delivered according to the direction thereon by the Postal Service, a written communication, postmarked at Palatine, Illinois, on March 10, 1997, addressed to William H. Gates III at Redmond, Washington, and containing a threat to injure the person of William H. Gates III, that is, to kill him.
>
> All in violation of Title 18, United States Code, Section 876.[11]

Pletcher, 22 years old, wrote to Gates at Microsoft demanding $5 million. Pletcher claimed he had killed people while in the military and could kill Gates "with one bullet from my rifle at a quarter of a mile away."[12]

Then Pletcher proposed an elaborate communication scheme that involved placing a personal ad on the

America Online "Netgirl" bulletin board. After a series of exchanges and escalated threats, Pletcher warned Gates that he must pay the extortion "to avoid dying, among other things." The letter included a diskette that Gates was to use to communicate with Pletcher.

By that time the FBI had traced the postmark on some of the letters and enlisted AOL's assistance in locating members in the most likely areas and in identifing some members using the Netgirl bulletin board. But the diskette was the clincher. Pletcher left his parents' name and Long Grove, Illinois, address on the diskette. After that it wasn't difficult to pick him up or to find out that he was wanted for other types of Internet fraud. Pletcher was soon behind bars, facing up to 20 years in prison and fines of $250,000 on four separate counts of mail extortion.

Pletcher's lawyers say that, despite the fact that he'd applied for a Luxembourg bank account, the young man never intended to get money from the extortion scheme and would not have injured Gates. "The evidence will show that he was playing out an imaginative scenario."

I don't think so, said the jury. In March 1998 Pletcher was convicted and sentenced to 70 months in prison plus three years in supervised release.[13]

∽

Gates does not like to discuss his wealth. In fact, he tries to pretend that he is not fabulously well off, as this 1990 interview suggests:

Reporter: What does all the money you have mean to you?

Gates: I don't have any money; I have stock. I own about 35 percent of the shares of Microsoft, and I take a salary of $175,000 a year.

Reporter: Yes, but you sold about $30 million worth of Microsoft stock, didn't you?

Gates: About a year ago.

Reporter: Most people still consider that "money." Don't you?

Gates: Yes, that's money . . . that's money.

Reporter: Now that we've established that you do have money, what does it mean to you?[14]

∽

Gates realizes that being wealthy is not a path to popularity:

"I don't think the rich get much credit for anything."[15]

STOCK MARKET ROLLER COASTER

In March 1998 Microsoft shares reached a total stock market valuation of more than $285 billion, a feat previously achieved only by General Electric. This made Microsoft the second most highly valued stock on the exchanges. On March 3, 1998, Microsoft stock split two for one—its seventh split since going public.

Microsoft had 2.4 billion shares outstanding before the split.

Over the past ten years Microsoft has given shareholders an average annual return of 45.6 percent, the highest return for that length of time of any publicly traded company. Warren Buffett's highly respected Berkshire Hathaway has given shareholders a return of only 31.6 percent during the same time.

Yet Gates was unimpressed:

"The company is a high-tech stock and high-tech stocks are volatile. The price is not a reflection of the contribution we make."[16]

~

When Gates said Microsoft's stock could be volatile, he meant it: In the October 1987 stock market crash, Gates's paper losses topped $350 million. In July 1995, in a period of several days, Gates lost $2 billion. This problem plagues many billionaires.

In 1997 the stock market in the United States was in its seventh bull year and, understandably, investors were skittish. They jumped out of their skins on Monday, October 27, when the market nosedived. The five richest Americans saw their holdings shrink by nearly $4 billion. By Tuesday the situation looked a lot better, as the stock holdings of Bill Gates, Warren Buffett, Paul Allen, Larry Ellison, and Gordon Moore rebounded by $3.6 billion. Here's the breakdown:

	MONDAY'S DROP	*TUESDAY'S REBOUND*
BILL GATES	$1.76 billion	$1.25 billion
WARREN BUFFETT, chairman, Berkshire Hathaway Corp.	$717.3 million	$765.2 million
PAUL ALLEN, co-founder, Microsoft Corp.	$600 million	$426.9 million
LARRY ELLISON, chairman, CEO and president, Oracle Corp.	$610.2 million	$681.1 million
GORDON MOORE, chairman, Intel Corp.	$236.2 million	$461.1 million

THE LAKE WASHINGTON ESTATES

In 1995 Gates celebrated his fortieth birthday by setting up a makeshift putting course on the yet-unfinished grounds of his Lake Washington estate. The 40,000-square-foot mansion should have been completed by then, but like other Microsoft products, it was finished late. Well, it was only a personal deadline. Gates could take all the time he wanted.

～

Work began on the house in 1990, and although Gates and his family moved in early in 1998, construction still was not finished. Work slowed when Gates got married, since his wife, Melinda, had ideas of her own. For example, she objected that Gates had a study and she did not.

~

In 1995 the King County Assessor's office sent an appraiser to the property. He reported back that the house was less complete than it was a year earlier, partly because the architects and technicians were learning as they went.

The appraiser said he wasn't yet sure how the house should be valued for tax purposes, since it would never be resold for the amount it cost to build. "We know now, and we knew last year, that the subject residence was not being built to market expectations."[17]

Originally expected to cost $35 million, the Gates estate to date is estimated at costing about $73 million—though some estimates run as high as $100 million.

Ultimately, the county assessed the estate at $53 million for tax purposes. This meant a $580,000 annual tax bill for Bill—255 times King County's average property tax bill of $2,275. Gates at first protested the assessment, but later dropped his complaint.[18]

~

Gates acquired the four-lot 4.5-acre property in the Puget Sound community of Medina gradually, buying the first parcel of land in 1988. The site was a challenge to architects because of its steep slope which drops 154 feet to the lake. A new home that stood on the site was sold for less than $100,000, jacked up, and barged up-lake to a new location.

~

"We want to do buildings that connect people to the land," said James Cutler, half of the architectural team that designed the Gates mansion.[19]

"People don't even make eye contact anymore," Cutler noted. "We're just floating. Whatever I can do to reconnect us to a place, to make you look around and think, 'This place is beautiful,' that's what I do."[20]

Cutler and his partner, Peter Bohlin of Wilkes-Barre, Pennsylvania, were able to experiment with their environmental ideas, including a zealousness for saving trees:

"With Gates, we've gone to lumber salvaged from demolished buildings—280,000 board feet, and it's all genuine salvage."[21]

The earthquake-resistant compound is constructed of 500-year-old Douglas fir timbers reclaimed from a Weyerhauser mill on the Columbia River. It has a stainless steel roof. The house is built into a hillside to minimize impact on the neighborhood and to conserve energy.

The Gates compound is approached through a massive guarded gate at the top of a curving, 1,000-foot-long private road. Near the bottom of the property there is another gate, a giant wooden wedge with doors large enough to accommodate a school bus.

A 1,700-square-foot guest house was completed first as a test house and a place for Gates to stay during construction.

Made up of five pavilions, the estate includes a lake-view dining room that seats 100, a game room, a 20-seat movie theater, and a 14,000-book library. The ornate library has a central dome, fireplace, and two secret pivoting bookcases, one of which hides a bar.

There also is a boathouse and dock, trampoline, and several parking areas, including a 100-car underground facility. Floors in the house and the driveways are heated.

The 17-by-60-foot swimming pool is piped with underwater music and the bottom is painted in a fossil motif. Swimmers can dive under a glass wall to go outside.

Gates's architects explained that visitors may never get a sense of the place where Gates actually lives, since the family compound is very isolated. The family area has bedrooms for three children. Altogether the house has 7 bedrooms, 24 bathrooms, 6 kitchens (1 commercial kitchen), and 6 fireplaces.

～

Rather than a lawn, the forest was replanted around the buildings. At first Gates was unhappy that Cutler wanted to turn 125 feet of the $20,000-a-foot waterfront property into wetlands—a swamp if you will. Cutler assured him, "You'll mark your life by the changes in this landscape. Your children will come to this place."[22]

The private estuary is stocked with (surprise?) cutthroat trout.

"I didn't want gee-whiz technology to be the home's defining characteristic. I wanted technology to play a role in a home that was handsome and practical and

livable. Growing up in the Northwest, I naturally wanted to create a setting that reflected the environment. We were lucky enough to find a good site for the home, and we've put a lot of care into making the home work well with the natural setting."[23]

~

When choosing an interior designer, the Gateses hired a local architect as an advisor, reviewed 500 slides of decorators' work, then sent letters to 25 candidates promising a fair decision and one that would reflect "taste and quality."[24]

NOTE: Thierry W. Despont became the interior designer.[25]

~

Guests are given a pin when they enter the house that allows their favorite music to follow them, their favorite works of art to appear on high-definition TV monitors, lights to go on and off when they enter and leave rooms, and telephone calls to be switched automatically to the nearest telephone. Guests also can go to the nearest computer terminal and select a movie or a television program, which will follow them to the nearest screen.

When Gates lounges around the house he most likely is followed by his favorite music from the 1940s and 1950s, especially Frank Sinatra.

In addition to world-class art on the television screens, Gates wanted live video from interesting places. Though there is no indication Gates uses these sites, such services are available, including a photo of a coffeepot at Oxford University in England and a constantly updated view of a bridge across the River Liffey in Dublin. Those who don't already have a view of Lake Washington can get a constantly renewed vista from a camera mounted on the University of Washington campus.

The coffeepot Internet address:
> http://www.cl.cam.ac.uk/coffee/coffee.html

Dublin bridge:
> http://www.Irish-Times.com/Irish-Times/Live/

The Lake Washington view:
> http://www.cac.washington.edu:1180

Gates's book *The Road Ahead* comes with a CD-ROM with a guided tour of his home.

~

When Gates first moved in, the high-density TV in his bedroom didn't work:

"It was just sitting there shining."[26]

He had to throw a blanket over the screen to get to sleep.

~

This isn't another San Simeon, insists Gates, not "one of the West Coast's monuments to excess."[27] Instead it is a house of the future, a test site for computer-assisted living.

~

Writer Margaret Talbot says Gates's home is the perfect symbol of the new elite. "It's not a monument to excess so much as a monument to control," she wrote.

For the Baby Boomer aristocracy " . . . control—over social reality, over the biological reality of reproduction and aging—has become an obsession. There are many ways to achieve this kind of mastery over one's environment, but Gates may have hit upon the surest: building yourself a technological cocoon that anticipates your every need and protects you not only from danger, but from serendipity as well."[28]

~

The long period of construction has been stressful for some neighbors:

"We had a quiet little dead-end street and all of a sudden this guy moves in and it changed the whole neighborhood," said William Richmond, who has lived on Lake Washington for 45 years.[29]

Richmond said that at least three families moved out during the eight-year construction process at Gates's home.

Apparently, Gates has tried to mitigate the annoyance by arranging for construction workers to wash dusty cars, equipment, and homes and to do free landscaping for neighbors. Audrey House, 92, who lives adjacent to the Gates property, appreciates the security guards and lights.

"You know you're safer here than if you lived down the street," House observed.[30]

~

John Cunningham, host of an on-line show called "Driveways of the Rich & Famous," caught Audrey in her driveway. Cunningham asked if she'd ever met Gates:

Audrey: Yes, ah-huh.

John: Oh, you have?

Audrey: He's a very fine man and he's been very good to me. They come around on Saturday and cut the lawn and that.

John: Oh really—he cuts your lawn?

Audrey: Not him, but he has a crew of men. And he's done a lot of other nice things around here.

John: So, you're pretty happy about having Mr. Gates as a neighbor?

Audrey: Oh yes, they're wonderful people.

Audrey said that because she's "crippled," she was unable to attend a party Gates gave for neighbors. But Melinda Gates promised to bring the baby over so Audrey could see her.[31]

~

Gates's house isn't the only Microsoft mansion on Lake Washington. Paul Allen's place includes three houses, a full-size gym, an indoor pool and water slide, and numerous garages. Steve Ballmer, his wife, Connie, and their two young sons live in a more modest 3,700-square-foot home on the lake.

~

Nathan Myhrvold, lead tech thinker for Microsoft, also is building a Lake Washington sanctuary about half a mile from the Gates estate. Myhrvold, who has tried various daring hobbies, now cooks. He's even studied with French chefs.

"With cooking, you're making something very tangible. Cleaning a duck or trussing a hog has a very earthy sort of appeal that you just can't get from technology."[32]

The centerpiece of his new home is a futuristic kitchen.

"Probably the closest thing to it is a three-star restaurant in Paris," Myhrvold says. "I say Paris because they have smaller kitchens."[33]

Don't worry that Gates and his friends are monopolizing the lakefront—Lake Washington is more than 25 miles long and is surrounded by thousands of homes.

~

The following passage from F. Scott Fitzgerald's *The Great Gatsby* is inscribed around the base of Gates's library dome: "He had come a long way to this blue lawn and his dream must have seemed so close he could hardly fail to grasp it."[34]

~

The Gates jesters suspect that God is jealous of Bill's estate:

"An executive of a major computing company died and went to heaven. While hanging around waiting for St. Peter to process him through, he noticed a very large, ultra-modern house with the initials 'B.G.' and a Microsoft logo emblazoned on the door. He was surprised because he hadn't heard that Bill Gates had died. 'Hey,' he said to St. Peter, 'is that Bill Gates's house?' St. Peter replied, 'Oh no, that's God's house. But sometimes he thinks he's Bill Gates.'"[35]

BILL'S CARS

"A fiendishly fast driver . . ."[36]

As a young man, Bill Gates seemed to collect speeding tickets for a hobby. He even got a ticket for racing in his power boat. With a taste for fast, glamorous cars, Gates used to let off steam late at night by driving fast on the highways of New Mexico and Washington states.

~

Although Gates says he's lightened up on the pedal in recent years, he was still getting citations after Microsoft moved its headquarters to Seattle. Some tickets were dismissed on technicalities, but at one point he was due in traffic court again and at risk of losing his driver's license.

He explained to business associate Seymour Rubinstein that the police officer may have given him a ticket because he had a radar detector in the car.

Gates planned to argue with the judge that he was within his rights to have the detector. Rubinstein convinced Gates to take another tack.

"I told Bill, 'You may be very well within your rights to have a radar detector in your fast Porsche. But the fact is they won't like it because they'll think the principal reason that you have it is to escape the law. The best thing for you to do is to tell them that you are going to throw away your radar detector, that you are really sorry about what you did, and that you are not going to speed anymore. Otherwise they are going to crush your nuts.'"[37]

Gates followed Rubenstein's counsel and got off with a fine.

~

If he's such a car guy, what does Gates drive?

High School: Red/orange Mustang convertible. At last report, he still had this car.

Early Microsoft: A blue Porsche 930 Turbo in Albuquerque. Gates once was taken to jail in Albuquerque for mouthing off to a highway patrolman, but friends bailed him out.

In recent years, Gates has owned a Jaguar XJ6, several Porsches including a $60,000 Carrera Cabriolet 964, a Ferrari 348, and a Lexus. In an attempt to cut down on speeding tickets, Gates once bought a brown diesel Mercedes Benz. He neglected to check the oil and burned up the engine.

~

Paul Allen persuaded Gates to join him in purchasing a pair of uncertified Porsche model 959s from a German citizen who brought them into the country. They bought the cars in the late 1980s for around $380,000 each, though at one time the model had been valued at $1 million. The car could go 170 mph. Gates drove his for much of 1989, then in 1990 the foreign citizen exemption expired. The roadster was not eligible for import to the United States since it did not meet U.S. emission or body-structure standards. Gates and Allen stored their cars in a free trade zone warehouse in Oakland, where presumably they remain today.

~

It may be no wonder that one of Microsoft's most popular Web sites is CarPoint (www.carpoint.com). The site offers dealer invoice prices on new models, a used-car value calculator from the *Kelley Blue Book*, buying tips, photos, and other information.

~

In an on-line forum, auto mechanics circulated a story about Gates and General Motors.

At a recent computer expo, Gates reportedly compared the computer industry to the auto industry. "If GM had kept up with technology like the computer industry has, we would all be driving $25 cars that get 1,000 miles per gallon."

GM shot back a reply: "Yes, but would you want your car to crash twice a day?"

One auto mechanic said he wouldn't want his car to crash at all, but if it did crash, he'd like to be able to fix it by closing the windows, getting out for a few seconds, restarting, and opening the windows.[38]

CHARITY BEGINS AT THE LIBRARY

When media mogul Ted Turner donated $1 billion to the United Nations, he challenged the world's wealthiest citizens, specifically Warren Buffett and Bill Gates, to match his generosity.

Gates told Barbara Walters in a *20/20* television interview that he felt he still had many years to live, build his wealth, and plan his own philanthropy:

"I'm very glad [Turner] has given that billion dollars. Certainly, my giving will be in the same league as Ted's—and beyond."[39]

~

"I'm in a phase for the next ten years where my work is my primary contribution. The idea of funding other things is some time off."[40]

~

Two months after Turner's dressing down, Gates gave $1.2 million worth of computer gear to six historically black colleges near Atlanta, Turner's home base. The software and hardware were given to Clark Atlanta University, Morehouse, Paine, Spelman, and Morris Brown colleges and the Interdenominational Theological Center. A spokesman for Gates said the contributions were not spurred by Turner's remarks.

"Bill's given away over $270 million. This is nothing new," said spokesman Greg Shaw. "This has nothing to do with Ted Turner."[41]

~

Gates was ranked fourth on *Fortune's* 1997 generosity list. Ted Turner was number one, thanks to his U.N. gift. Gates's contributions that year came to $210 million. Also generous, in 1996 Paul Allen gave $32 million to his favorite causes.

NOTE: For more about Microsoft's and Gates's charitable giving, log on to www.microsoft.com/corpinfo.

~

Lakeside School naturally called one of their most successful alumni when it was raising funds for a new building:

"How much is everyone else giving?" Gates asked.

"About $75," he was told.

"Put me down for $75," Gates replied.[42]

Just kidding. Gates and Allen anted up $2.2 million for a math and science facility, Allen Gates Hall.

~

Occasionally, a small but important cause catches Gates's attention. Residents of Glenvil, Nebraska (population 270), collected soda cans and held sports tournaments, trying to raise $20,000 to convert a former school playground into a park. The fund-raising committee also solicited Bill Gates and other wealthy people requesting contributions, explaining that Glenvil children needed a place to gather and to help fend off pressure to use drugs and alcohol.

Gates sent a check for $5,000 with a letter saying that he generally doesn't respond to pleas for money but was impressed with the committee's pitch.

"These problems are no longer big city problems," Gates wrote. "They are also becoming an alarming problem in rural communities."[43]

Gates requested a tax-exemption number, which the committee obligingly sent.

～

Libraries often benefit from Gates's charitable giving. He provided $12 million for a law school library at the University of Washington to be named for his father.

In 1997 Bill and Melinda Gates established the Gates Library Foundation, which will disburse $200 million of Gates's own money and $200 million in Microsoft software to public libraries in the United States. When that $400 million is combined with the $15 million Microsoft already contributed to a project called Libraries OnLine, Gates's largesse nears that of Andrew Carnegie, who gave $41.2 million for new library construction between 1890 and 1917. Carnegie's contribution would amount to $505 million in 1997 dollars.

Gates gave more money for libraries in 1997 than any single donor, including the federal government.

He believes that public libraries are fundamental institutions to American society and democracy and he hopes to bridge the gap between those who have access to vital information and those who do not.

It is his goal to wire every library in every economically disadvantaged community, urban or rural, to the Internet by the year 2002. The $400 million contribution should make it possible to wire roughly half of the 16,000 U.S. public libraries.

"Since I was a kid, libraries have played an important role in my life. In the past couple of years I have had the opportunity to visit many libraries and see firsthand how people are using personal computers and the Internet to do anything from looking for a job to researching a term paper."[44]

~

Gates hopes library computers will encourage older Americans to explore the Net, thus narrowing the gap between generations:

"I grew up during the Vietnam War, which among other things pitted one generation against another in the United States. I've seen the turmoil that exists when one generation, or one portion of our society, perceives the world quite differently than another."[45]

~

Critics called Gates's donation "a down payment on the purchase of public libraries." They complained that half the contribution was Microsoft software, which would obligate libraries to buy Microsoft products in the future. Not so, according to Gates:

> *"Microsoft will continue to give all the software away for this program. The money I'm giving, the $200 million, is hard cash to help buy communications, training, and support all the pieces that go into this. Microsoft is giving software to the library market, and anyone else is welcome to give software to the library market."*[46]

Bill Gates, Sr., administers the approximately $300-million William H. Gates III Foundation. Bill III says he will give away 95 percent of his wealth before he dies.[47]

> *"Spending money intelligently is as difficult as earning it. Giving away money in meaningful ways will be a main preoccupation later in my life— assuming I still have a lot to give away."*[48]

> *"Eventually I'll return most of [my money] as contributions to causes I believe in, such as education and population stability."*[49]

> *"One thing is for sure. I won't leave a lot of money to my heirs because I don't think it would be good for them."*[50]

In addition to Gates's personal giving, Microsoft also is involved in charitable activities. In 1997, the company donated more than $14 million in cash and $45 million in software to charitable and nonprofit groups. Microsoft also launched a $7 million initiative with the nation's community colleges. The goal of Working Connections is to train more people for information technology careers.

$\sim$

Gates did not have an assigned parking place at Microsoft until panhandlers pestered him so much he finally needed a more protected spot. But Gates listens to some beggars:

> *"Last week I went out to dinner. Someone came up to me, asking me for money. I wasn't sure what to do. Then he said that I should look up his home page, and gave me his URL. I didn't know if it was true or not, but it was such a good line I gave the guy five bucks. So he may be a homeless person with a home page."*[51]

PIE IN THE FACE

As Gates arrived for a meeting with business and government leaders in Brussels, a prankster slammed a big, sticky cream pie in his face. Television networks worldwide immediately started bidding, some paying as much as $4,000, for film of the assault. Gates took the incident gracefully, except for complaining that the pie didn't taste good.

The pie was tossed by a group calling itself "a gang of bad hellions" who have declared war on all the "unpleasant celebrities" of the world. They are led by Belgian author, film historian, and actor Noel Godin, who describes himself as an "entarteur," or pie-ist.

Why slather Gates?

"Because," explained Godin, "in a way he is the master of the world, and then because he's offering his intelligence, his sharpened imagination and his power to governments and to the world as it is today—that is to say gloomy, unjust and nauseating. He could have been a Utopist, but he prefers being the lackey of the establishment."[52]

Godin said his group are comic terrorists and their acts are symbolic. They did not toss their cream concoction at the urging of Gates's enemies.

"We have never been pie mercenaries," Godin insisted.[53]

The pie-throwing event sent Internet comedians on a tear:

One Web site ran a satirical interview with the pie herself, who would identify herself only as "Monica." She denied that she was an "apple pie."

Furthermore, "She laughed off any suggestion that 'pie' stood for 'pull Internet Explorer.' However, her hardened pastry shell showed some cracks when we pointed out that 'pi' is the sixteenth letter in the Greek alphabet and that 'Internet Explorer' has 16 letters in it."[54]

LITTLE TIME
FOR LOVE

SINGLE IN SEATTLE

" . . . something of a ladies man . . ."[1]

Nothing fascinates like a wealthy bachelor, and Gates was no exception. The gossip flew about his exploits when he was single, though some stories were little more than rumors.

~

Gates described his experience with "virtual dating" when he and a girlfriend were working in different cities. They would select a movie that was playing in both their cities, talk about it on their car phones as they drove to the theater, watch the movie separately, then talk again on the drive home. Apparently, it wasn't a fully satisfying experience. The romance finally ended.

~

In 1984 *Time* magazine printed a cozy picture of Gates with his then-girlfriend, Jill Bennett. Bennett sold computers for Digital Equipment. Then for several years

Gates dated computer industry analyst Ann Winblad.

Raised in a small town in Minnesota, Winblad was a high school cheerleader and financed her college education serving cocktails. She started a software company with $500, selling it several years later for $15.5 million. Winblad bought a San Francisco Victorian mansion, then cofounded a venture capital firm with former National Basketball Association center John Hummer. They struggled to raise $35 million in capital in 1989, but by 1996 had escalated the investment pool to $260 million. So far they've delivered a 50 percent average annual return to investors. She and Gates remain friends. When Gates and his fiancée, Melinda, toured Africa, Winblad was among a group of friends who went along.

~

"He's always been married to Microsoft," said Estelle Mathers, Gates's former administrative assistant.[2]

~

"It certainly took me a lot of time, being a single person."[3]

~

When Gates became a billionaire at age 31, his former office manager, Miriam Lubow, teased him about all the offers of marriage he would now receive. But Gates was too busy to think about marriage:

"When I'm 35, I'll get married."[4]

NOTE: Gates did not marry until he was 38.

WEDDING SONG

Playboy magazine asked Gates why he got married:

> *"There's some magic there that's hard to describe, and I'm pursuing that."*

"Can you describe how Melinda makes you feel?" asked the interviewer.

> *"Amazingly, she made me feel like getting married. Now that is unusual! It's against all my past rational thinking on the topic."[5]*

～

Gates met Melinda French, a mid-level Microsoft executive who grew up in Dallas and attended a Catholic girls' school, at a company picnic in 1987. Apparently, he was attracted to her because she is independent, smart, and funny. Nine years Bill's junior, Melinda is a runner with an MBA. The couple dated for six years.

～

Gates's mother Mary, who was battling breast cancer, encouraged Bill to get married. She liked Melinda and thought it was about time her son settled down.

After Gates proposed to French in 1993, he secretly diverted a chartered plane they were taking home from Palm Springs to Omaha, Nebraska. There they were met by Warren Buffett, who escorted them to Borsheim's jewelry store (owned by Buffett's Berkshire Hathaway Inc.) to select an engagement ring.

"Not to give you advice or anything," said Buffett, who is known for the unabashed promotion of his own companies, "but when I bought an engagement ring for my wife in 1951, I spent 6 percent of my net worth on it." Gates already was a multibillionaire and six percent of his net worth would have been around $500 million.[6]

~

At an engagement party given for Bill and Melinda by Silicon Valley friends, Bill dressed as The Great Gatsby and Melinda dressed as Daisy Buchanan.[7]

~

The rumors regarding the Gates-French prenuptial agreement are so torrid that they alone could account for global warming. Warren Buffett thinks they are nothing but rumor: "I would bet my life that Bill and Melinda do not have a prenuptial or for that matter [a] postnuptial agreement."[8]

~

On New Year's Day, 1994, French and Gates were married in a lavish $1-million seaside Roman Catholic ceremony on the Hawaiian island of Lanai. The bride wore a $10,000 white silk-faced organza wedding dress by Seattle designer Victoria Glenn. Gates wore a white dinner jacket and black slacks. Among the celebrities attending were *Washington Post* publisher Katharine Graham and four billionaires—Warren Buffett, Paul

Allen, Steve Ballmer, and cellular telephone magnate Craig McCaw.

During the week of the wedding celebration, Gates reportedly booked all the hotel rooms on Lanai and hired all the helicopters on Maui to keep photographers from snooping.

Even *Washington Post* reporters were barred, though Kay Graham was a guest. "They really wanted a private, human wedding and they didn't want publicity. They didn't want people with cameras and notebooks. I respected their wishes."[9]

⌣

Other journalists were not so respectful. Although most of the island of Lanai is the private property of Dole Food Co., some beaches are public. However, private security guards and local Lanai police intercepted reporters on a public beach and made them leave the island. A Seattle television reporter was arrested, even though he had broken no law. Using his own money, Scott Rensberger of KIRO-TV sued. In a private settlement, Rensberger got letters of apology from Dole and Microsoft and a $127,000 donation to projects for residents of Lanai.

"I was prepared to go to trial," Rensberger said, "I spent almost all of my life savings to put myself up here in the hope that a jury would say, 'Yes, you're right.'"[10]

⌣

"Microsoft competitors are sometimes quoted in the press as hoping that married life will somehow make

*me less competitive, perhaps by distracting me from
my work. After two years of marriage, that hasn't
happened, and I don't think it will anytime soon."[11]*

~

Gates's idea of relaxation is to race Melinda in assembling identical jigsaw puzzles.[12]

~

Melinda Gates continued to work at Microsoft after the wedding. She values her privacy so much she wrote to former schools and neighbors, asking them not to talk about her to the media. Even her mother was asked to remain mum:

"I was told that if you need any information, you should call Microsoft," explained Elaine French to a reporter.[13]

~

To one reporter who requested an interview, Melinda Gates wrote: "While I understand that your readers may find my story interesting because of the man I married, it is a personal decision for me not to share information about our relationship or my personal life with the world at large."[14]

On the eve of Gates's testimony before a Senate committee investigating antitrust charges against Microsoft, Bill and Melinda rendezvoused at a Washington, D.C., hotel. Gates wrote this account of their meeting in his *Slate* magazine on-line dairy:

"We walked up Pennsylvania Avenue from the hotel so I could show her the boardinghouse I stayed in when I was a page in Congress. We walked up the steps of the Capitol. I showed her the flagpole where they run flags up and down all day so they can send flags to people all over the United States mentioning that they flew over the United States Capitol. We went into the National Gallery and saw some paintings by one of our favorite artists—Hopper. We had a quick pizza for dinner."[15]

Melinda Gates joined her husband the following day when he testified before the Senate Judiciary Committee to defend Microsoft's business practices.

"TWINKLE, TWINKLE, LITTLE STAR"

Jennifer Katharine Gates was born to Bill, 40, and Melinda, 31, on April 26, 1996, in Bellevue, Washington. She arrived shortly after 6 P.M. and weighed in at 8 pounds 6 ounces.

∼

When Bill Gates was interviewed early in 1998 by Barbara Walters for *20/20*, she asked him to sing his daughter's favorite lullaby, "Twinkle, Twinkle, Little Star." Gates obliged. Partway into the song Walters cut him off, "Okay, that's enough." Gates took it calmly.

"I wasn't asked in advance to sing that song . . . but Melinda and I have been taking singing lessons, so in that sense it was fine. Interviews often are full

of surprises. Connie Chung once asked me to jump over a chair in my office. I did that, too."[16]

~

It came as a surprise to some that Gates would want to have children. After all, he was once said to have pointed at an infant and stated, "That scares me."[17]

> *"I knew I'd enjoy parenthood, so that part isn't a surprise, but I guess it surprises me just how much fun it really is. Jennifer loves the computer. She calls it a 'puter.' She loves books even more, which is healthy. She looks like me and she looks like Melinda. She has a definite personality, which I would say is distinctly her own."*[18]

~

> *"For me, I love the idea that most nights I get a chance to go home early and see my young daughter; but after she goes to bed, then I'm back down in my den checking electronic mail, answering the questions people have had through the course of the day and putting down my thoughts."*[19]

~

> *". . . I love using Barney software with my 18-month-old daughter. Now, I constantly find myself humming Barney's song. In fact, I can't even say the word 'computer' in my house, because if she hears me say it, she'll just start saying, 'puter, puter, puter,' and she won't do anything until I take her and let her play with that. And that really is a lot of fun."*[20]

~

At a 1998 college seminar, Gates was asked about his personal goals for the next ten years. Gates fumbled around for a moment, then the moderator asked, "Is that in your PC?"

"I'm sure it's in here somewhere. I just have to download it. Ask my wife what she has to say. You know, in my personal life I don't set big goals. I'm sure ten years from now, I'll probably have a couple more kids, because I'm enjoying having a daughter who's almost two years old now. That's the most fun thing I've ever done, and look forward to more."[21]

~

Gates's lullaby to Jennifer, as imagined by *Advertising Age* columnist Bob Garfield:

"Hush little baby, don't say a word, Pappa's gonna buy you a mockingbird. And if that mockingbird don't sing, Pappa's gonna buy you . . . Oh, I don't know . . . Europe?"[22]

THE NEW COMPUTER CULTURE

KIDS AND COMPUTERS

"When I look at what technology is beginning to offer children, I wish I were a kid again."[1]

~

"If a kid is addicted to a personal computer, I think that's far better than watching TV, because at least his mind is making choices. I'm not one of those people who hates TV, but I don't think it exercises your mind much."[2]

~

Gates says that unlike the group experience of television, computers are a personal activity that allows children to explore their own interests.

"I'm one of those people who thinks kids ought to learn how to multiply with a pencil and paper even though calculators can do it for them. But at the same time, I have no doubts that computers can help kids develop more of their mental potential."[3]

"Somewhere around two, three, or four is when kids should begin computing. Kids love interactivity, and they love that surprise element. The first time [they clicked], they didn't know something was there; the second time, they thought they remembered it; the third time, they're pretty sure; the fourth time, they think they're in control . . . they're willing to go back and explore those spaces and just get a kick out of it."[4]

"Computers are a lot like books when they were first utilized. Initially they are used only by a narrow set of people but to the advantage of everybody—for example, medical researchers.

"But what you really want is to have a concept of computer literacy like you have for normal literacy. You can achieve this, for example, by providing every library with a PC that is linked to the Internet. As part of your school curriculum, you should be exposed to the Internet."[5]

"I was out at a very poor elementary school today, and these fifth-graders were telling me how they build Web sites, and they're actually funding the technology being used at their school by going to local businesses and doing Web sites for them. So you've got to watch out for these fifth-graders. They've got printing presses in the forms of personal computers, and they're very creative in what they're doing."[6]

Gates sees computers as life-enhancing tools. He has worked with immigrant children from Bosnia and believes that computers helped them adjust to a new home:

> *"The silent objectivity of the computer allows children to reconcile issues surrounding the integration to America. It endowed these immigrant children with the power to present their view of today's world. It is this personal viewpoint which serves as an importation for Americans old and new."[7]*

Gates once said that if he had children, he would not allow them to explore the Internet unsupervised. The World Wide Web has much important and fascinating information, but it also contains lies, rantings and ravings, and pornography:

> *"The world has never had a global publishing vehicle before. It is not always clear who should be held accountable when something is published improperly—whether because it is copyrighted, proprietary, defamatory or pornographic. Old rules and distinctions don't apply."[8]*

Although Gates says he would like to protect children from pornography, he is wary of laws that restrict free speech on the Internet.

"Both the Bill of Rights and the Internet are potentially fragile. Mess with either of them too much, and we might ruin them."[9]

~

When Gates visited Canada and demonstrated children's software about to come off the Microsoft assembly line, Canadians got the impression that Microsoft didn't intend to change the culture much, at least as far as boy/girl stereotypes are concerned:

"One [virtual reality game] teaches visitors to Horrorland how to appease a meat-eating plant with chunks of animal flesh. Another was about cooking, designed, he said, for girls, who lag behind boys in their interest in computer games. In the virtual world according to Gates, the girls' place is in the kitchen," explained a reporter.[10]

~

Much of the e-mail Gates gets is from children:

"But a surprisingly high percentage also comes from senior citizens, people who have taken the time to get knowledgeable about the technology, and they're really out there contributing to chat sessions, trying to find things that can really engage them."[11]

BOOKS ARE NOT OBSOLETE

A blizzard put the power out and drove writer Lance Morrow away from his computer: "I found myself wishing that a hard snow would fall on Seattle. Bill Gates and his geek brigades, I thought, need to sit in the dark for a while, or to light oil lamps and catch up on their reading."[12]

Actually, Gates may share that wish. He tries to get in an hour or more of reading each weeknight and a few hours each weekend. He reads the newspaper every day and several magazines a week.

"I make it a point to read at least one news weekly from cover to cover, because it broadens my interests. If I only read what intrigues me, such as the science section and a subset of the business section, then I finish the magazine the same person I was before I started. So I read it all."[13]

~

Among Gates's favorite books are *The Great Gatsby*, *The Catcher in the Rye*, and *A Separate Peace*. He also enjoyed *The Bridges of Madison County*.[14] Among business books, Gates recommends Alfred P. Sloan, Jr.'s *My Years at General Motors*. On his trip to Africa several years ago, Gates read *Lucy* by Don Johanson and Maitland Edey, about a 3.5-million-year-old skeleton they had discovered. Gates more recently read *A Lesson Before Dying* by Ernest J. Gaines and *The Shipping News* by E. Annie Prouix.

~

An avid reader, Gates doesn't mind delays when he's traveling because it gives him an opportunity to read.

Gates says he carries around more books than he will ever be able to get to:

"There are books that have been around the globe more than once and haven't been opened."[15]

~

Gates doesn't expect computers to replace books, since books have physical characteristics that make them both useful and endearing. But he says children can treasure software in the same way they do books:

"My kids will have computers, of course. But they will have books first."[16]

~

Gates gave himself three to four months to write his book *The Road Ahead.* At the end of that time he and his coauthors, Nathan Myhrvold and Peter Rinearson, threw out what they had written and started over.

"My admiration for people who write books has increased now that I've done one myself. Writing a nonfiction book forces you to really think issues through in a disciplined way. It challenges you to order your thoughts. You find hidden gaps and inconsistencies, which prompts still more thought."[17]

LIVING THE INTERNET LIFESTYLE

More than 4,000 Russians crowded into the Kremlin in the fall of 1997 to hear Bill Gates talk about the Internet.

"I think in a decade from now, most people will use the Web many times each day. They will take it for granted, like we use the telephone today."[18]

Gates told the Russians that the Internet will link them to the world:

"People don't have to move. They don't have to change where they are in order to make their skills available to customers on a global basis. This is the opposite of brain drain. This is 'brain retention,' along with incredible opportunities for people with strong educational backgrounds, which you know this country has a great deal of."[19]

~

No one knows exactly how many people use the Internet, but according to some estimates, 38 million people worldwide are now able to log on.[20]

"Despite the Web's surging usage, nobody really lives a Web lifestyle yet—and won't, fully, until computers turn on instantly, network connections work faster, software is easier, and people have lost their apprehension about computers and Internet security. But these developments will all happen reasonably soon."[21]

~

Within ten years, however, most Americans will take the Internet lifestyle for granted.

"What I mean by that is that they exchange electronic mail with their friends and relatives. They are able to stay in touch with their kids who are off at school a lot better through electronic mail. If they want to do something major, like buy a car, they can go to the Internet and find out exactly what their dealer paid for that car. So, they're a little smarter when they go in to do that negotiation. Information of all types is out there, and they just take it for granted that they can go and get that."[22]

⁓

Gates says the Internet revolution gets an enormous amount of attention, especially when compared to the PC revolution.

"There were a few people who believed in it. We'd get together and say, 'Aren't we right about this? Aren't we going to overthrow those big computers? You know, we'll show everybody.' We felt like people weren't paying enough attention. Well, this revolution is the opposite of that. People are almost paying too much attention."[23]

⁓

Before his daughter was born, Gates used the Internet to research childbirth, and he gave his family digital, filmless cameras at Christmas so they can swap photos across the Internet.[24]

⁓

197

"I buy books through Amazon [an on-line book-store] because time is short and they have a big inventory and they've been very reliable. I'm surprised that videotapes aren't out there yet. I'm sure someone will come along and offer that. Maybe I'm the only one who wants that."[25]

~

Knowing that the Internet can be a rude, crude, angry place, Gates minds his manners:

"I comb my hair every time before I send e-mail hoping to appear attractive. I try to use punctuation in a friendly way also. I send :) and never :("[26]

~

"I have to say I feel sorry for the President of the United States, because I get copied on a lot of messages that are sent to him—and I think he probably has a tougher time getting through his e-mail even than I do."[27]

~

Gates says it is essential for businesses to be on the Internet because customers expect a high level of service:

"Customers expect, when they call in, for you to immediately be able to see your history of working with that customer and understand what they're doing. In many cases, the customer wants to be able to

*call up any time of the day, any day of the week, and
be connected in and see what the status of their order
is, or see any messages that you might have. Having
an Internet site gives you that total capability."*[28]

⁓

*"Ah, yes, my favorite Web site, People Against Poodles.
Everybody is entitled to their opinion. There's the
poor little dog—cute pooch or ambassador of evil?
And this is [a] very sophisticated Web site. Why Pooh-
pooh must die."*[29]

Relax, dog lovers. Gates uses the poodle Web site just
to illustrate how many different forms of expression
can be found on the Internet.

⁓

Newspaper publishers asked Gates if computers would
change newspapers.

*"But it's like saying, 'will plays be different after
movies?' or 'will TV be different?' I mean, the medi-
ums don't change just because a new medium comes
in. People like the newspapers today. They like what
they do with it."*[30]

⁓

However, e-mail could make telephone numbers obsolete:

*"An evolution of today's e-mail names will be what
you use to get in touch with somebody, whether you*

want to initiate a voice call, send a message or beep their beeper. First you'll indicate whom you want to contact, selecting from a personal address book or from a large directory, and then you'll choose what kind of contact you want. Software will take care of the rest."[31]

~

While the Internet has great promise, it also has problems, some trivial and others serious:

"When I went to a movie the other night, before the movie, they had one of those ads that they decided to run in advance and one of them had a URL that was about 90 characters long. And people in the audience were laughing. I'm not sure why they were laughing. Was it because it was 90 characters long, or it just appeared so foreign with all those dots and slashes and everything? But you know, it was better than the movie that came afterward."[32]

~

Another problem is that the Internet can't always be trusted.

"[Internet] security is a particular issue for me, because about 90 percent of the electronic mail on the Internet that appears to come from me does not come from me. So, if you get sort of an unsolicited job offer, rude statements coming to you, you might think twice about whether that's really me out there

sending that mail. There's some people who send me
mail that says, 'thank you for visiting our site; do you
like our site? Isn't it a wonderful site?' Of course I've
never heard of your site. I'm not quite sure what to
say back. I don't want to disappoint people."[33]

~

Bill Gates chain mail, pitch letters, and other bogus communications proliferate on the Internet. No matter how obvious the letters are, they always seem to catch a few fish. In February 1998 an e-mail signed by Gates went out to hundreds of college students, offering $1,000 in cash or a free copy of Windows 98 if the recipients would forward the message to 1,000 people and test some new software. Hundreds of students contacted Microsoft in response to the phony e-mail, demanding their $1,000. None, apparently, demanded a free copy of Windows 98.[34]

~

Web surfers show up for Bill, even when they know it's not the real Gates. A Bill Gates impersonator appeared on the Hecklers Online (HO) area of America Online. The chat room is devoted to "cracking jokes and doing things you can get away with only in cyberspace." From 450 to 460 attendees crowded into the on-line chat room to talk to the fake Gates. Even on-line, 450 people make a lot of noise when they're in one room.[35]

~

Gates may be annoyed by on-line hoaxters, but he is more worried about keeping saboteurs off the Internet.

> *"A complete failure of the information highway is worth worrying about. Because the system will be thoroughly decentralized, any single outage is unlikely to have a widespread effect. If an individual server fails, it will be replaced and its data restored. But the system could be susceptible to assault. As the system becomes more important, we will have to design in more redundancy."[36]*

Some people think Microsoft itself is the greatest threat to the freedom of the Internet. Indeed, Gates himself envisions a powerful position.

> *"The Information Highway will generate a higher volume of transactions than anything has to date, and we're proposing that Windows be at the center, servicing all those transactions."[37]*

Yet Gates says Microsoft is not trying to dominate the Internet.

> *" . . . it is not, nor has it ever been, the intention of my company to turn the information superhighway into a toll road."[38]*

Furthermore, says Gates: "Nobody controls the Internet and nobody ever will. That's the great thing about it. It's the most democratic, level playing field for commerce and the exchange of ideas and information that has ever existed."[39]

"The beauty of the Internet is its openness. It cannot be controlled or dominated or cut off, because it is simply a constantly changing series of linkages. It is such a creative, living medium that no one yet fully comprehends its opportunities."[40]

～

Gates would like to see the Internet free of government intervention (though it was a government invention in the first place), but some restrictions are inevitable:

" . . . I think it's very unlikely that institutions like the Securities and Exchange Commission are going to let people do offerings on the Internet without looking at the honesty of the material that's being promoted. It is unlikely the Federal Trade Commission will let people scam buyers without looking into that. Laws related to libel or copyright and those things probably will have to be accommodated. But it's a very difficult accommodation, because we haven't really defined modes of behavior, and we haven't dealt with the fact that this is a global network. It's going to be a terrible problem if there are overly restrictive laws that really prevent people from taking advantage of it."[41]

～

One conduit of unsolicited and often offensive e-mail is Hotmail, a free e-mail that was acquired by Microsoft:

> "Hotmail is one of the leaders in the fight against unsolicited commercial and otherwise undesirable e-mail messages. In fact, nearly one third of its customer service organization is dedicated to protecting Hotmail members from receiving such unwanted and offensive e-mail, and to tracking and disabling Hotmail members who use their accounts in this manner. This staff monitors lists of known spammers and offenders, and blocks all mail from these sources from entering the system. In addition, each account is able to set filters and has a special 'block sender' function that will route any future messages from a given address to the Trash Can.
>
> "Hotmail has taken numerous actions to combat this problem—including technological, policy, and legislative measures. For example, Hotmail is a strong supporter of CAUCE—the Coalition Against Unsolicited Commercial E-mail—and meets monthly with CAUCE and the FTC to determine the most effective ways to significantly reduce the flow of spam across the Web.
>
> "As a result of Hotmail's proactive measures the service has reduced offensive and unsolicited e-mail to a very small percentage of overall e-mail traffic. In fact, Hotmail estimates that more than 99 percent of offensive messages do not actually originate

*from the hotmail.com domain, but instead contain a
fake 'return address.'*

*"Unfortunately, sending out thousands of mes-
sages with forged '@hotmail.com' return addresses
is technically easy to do, and can be done from any
Internet service provider, and is a common means
for spammers to conceal their true identities. Hotmail recently took eight such offenders to court, and
as of this writing, has won its first preliminary
injunction against one of the defendants. Any recipi-
ent of offensive or nuisance e-mail messages should
forward them to abuse@hotmail.com."*[42]

～

Gates has endorsed an Internet Charter proposed
by European Commission regulators. The charter,
which will not be legally binding, lays down a set
of principles governing such areas as content, network security, encryption, and data protection. If
adopted, the charter will be used to influence and co-
ordinate laws in the 15 countries that comprise the
European Union. Each government will retain the
freedom to protect local laws, habits, and cultures
as it sees fit.

When we become an Internet society:

*"The concept that 'I belong to this nation' won't hold
as much sway with individuals as it once did. In
many ways, this is a good thing, particularly in
terms of being able to access expertise anywhere
in the world or finding others who share your com-*

mon interests. In terms of protecting cultural values, it may well be threatening. We may end up with less distinct cultures than we once had, and that is unfortunate."⁴³

~

There is an amazing amount of on-line material about Bill Gates. At the official Microsoft.com site you will find Gates's *New York Times* syndicated column, read about the company, or send Gates messages. His address is billg@microsoft.com. To read Gates's diary, log on to *Slate* on-line magazine. The magazine originally was free, but now there is a charge.

Another site touts his book, *The Road Ahead*. At Team Gates, a fan club site, you can buy Bill Gates T-shirts.

Some Web sites show how fanatical and frightening on-line activity can be. Sample headlines: "Bill Gates Dies in a Car Accident," "Proof that Bill Gates Is the Devil Himself," and "Never Trust a Billionaire."

Bill Gates Personal Wealth Clock calculates how much money you would get if Gates's wealth was handed out evenly to every citizen of the United States. Watch Bill's House Grow has photos by a Seattle resident who took his boat out on the lake and snapped construction pictures.

The Secret Diary of Bill Gates is not to be confused with Gates's official diary on *Slate*. The author of *The Secret Diary* posts this warning as a P.S. on his opening Web page.

"Bill Gates's lawyers think you might be confused

about who wrote this diary. Is it the REAL Bill Gates? Hmmmmm . . . I know you're WAY too smart to fall for it. But, hey, read my disclaimer anyway."[44]

COMPUTERS AND DEMOCRACY

Computers, the Internet, and Web TV may change the way our democracy works.

"Say the president goes on TV and asks everybody, 'What's your opinion on this?' That's a lot of messages coming in and that's gotta work."[45]

∽

While instant polls are possible, Gates isn't sure they are desirable.

"Someone will doubtless propose total 'direct democracy,' having all issues put to a vote, instead of our current representative democracy. Personally, I don't think direct voting would be a good way to run government."[46]

Gates says the average citizen may not have the time and resources to study every issue; therefore, a middleman—an elected representative—adds value to the process by doing the work for people.

∽

When asked what he thought of the Newt Gingrich theory that interactive networks would enable the overthrow of the liberal, secular media, Gates replied:

"It is a very strange notion that in a capitalistic economy the media somehow distorts the message. People on every end of the political spectrum can certainly feel that way. But it is hard to understand why there would be a systematic bias. After all, the owners of the media have the sole aim of seeking to give their audience what they want in a relatively competitive environment."[47]

～

Early in 1998 Gates and Microsoft were under attack from many quarters. *PC World Online* asked its readers how they felt about Gates.

"We received 2,900 responses in two days. While many responded to our survey with severe criticism of Gates and Microsoft, an equal number told us that Gates was their role model or their hero, and that Microsoft shouldn't be penalized for being successful."[48]

Twenty percent said they would vote for Gates if he ran for president in the year 2000.

COMPUTERS AND CAPITALISM

The trouble with capitalism, Gates says, is that there isn't enough of it.[49]

～

As the new millennium arrives, Gates predicts that about 80 percent of the economies of developing countries will be deeply affected by information technology. Where will poor countries find the money to gear themselves up for a computer-linked world? Although governments must participate by laying down infrastructure, Gates says capitalism has wondrous powers to mediate the gap between rich and poor:

"I guess it shows my faith in capitalism, but I believe middlemen will emerge who will find ways to equip Bangladesh with hardware and bring in the software so that they can take a 10 percent fee on the service work that those people will provide to the rest of the world and for themselves."[50]

~

"The United States has been the country that has embraced computer technology more rapidly than any other country, and it's no coincidence that the U.S. economy has benefitted from that and created more jobs than any other economy. There will be increasing competition here, and we want to make sure that we watch carefully the great work that will be done in Asia, India, China, Japan, Korea, Taiwan; all of these countries are really focused on this computer revolution and their companies are investing very heavily. If we're smart about this, we can cooperate with them, and the companies here will maintain a very strong position."[51]

~

Still, even a highly capitalistic country such as the United States has difficulty letting economic barriers fall. Gates says U.S. software makers cannot compete abroad in the encryption business because of limits that are promoted by the FBI and other law enforcement agencies here but not used by other governments:

> *"To date, we've had a huge problem, because we can't export decent encryption. We're stuck at 40 bits, which is easy to break. And foreign software competitors are shipping lots of 128-bit software. So our customers outside the U.S. say, 'Hey, you're providing us inferior products.' And we have to say, 'Well, it would be a felony to provide you with decent encryption.'"[52]*

It's not just a business issue.

> *"It is an issue of embracing the Information Age, which other countries have done. And it's an issue about civil liberties."[53]*

~

Although computers will reduce the number of paperwork jobs, the industry will create more jobs in certain sectors of employment:

> *"Most of the new jobs will result from society being richer as a result of overall production. Better medicine, more leisure time and better teaching are some of the areas on which I think society will focus its increased wealth."[54]*

~

"Today if you had to guess somebody's approximate income and you were limited to asking one polite question, a good one would be: 'What country do you live in?' That's because of the huge disparities in average wages from country to country.

"But a generation from now, if you want to guess someone's income, a more telling single question might be: 'What's your education?'"[55]

Computer literacy will be one of the characteristics of an educated person.

~

"The world of business is moving faster and faster and it's increasingly global. Using these digital systems to keep everybody in touch and analyze information in a rich way will be critical to the success of businesses in the future."[56]

~

Gates was asked when we would see a female Bill Gates, meaning a woman who started a company and attained Gates's level of wealth and influence:

"Well, nobody can predict these things. I mean, I didn't predict my success; how can I predict anyone else's? But high tech will involve more women because it is becoming more consumer-oriented and because it's a growth business that really needs to reach out to a broad set of talents."[57]

211

~

In a letter to the editors of *Time* magazine, former Microsoft employee Jeff James of Brookhaven, Pennsylvania, said he has seen how the company uses the concepts of capitalism, including survival of the fittest, aggressive action, and flexibility. "Like capitalism itself, these traits aren't always pretty, but they lead to success. Microsoft is by no means perfect; the company has left a history of big mistakes. But the never-say-die attitude, combined with Gates's vision of a world with no informational barriers, has led to where it is today."[58]

GATES ON LIFE

ON HUMAN INTELLIGENCE

If Gates could have the answer to one mystery, he
would ask how the human brain works:

> *"I'm in awe of the brain and its ability to learn. I'm
> fascinated by such things as how a child picks up lan-
> guages, by mental disorders such as autism, and by
> the role of the limbic brain in letting aromas trigger
> mood changes."[1]*

> *"I am always fascinated by the question of whether
> the most talented people end up in critical posi-
> tions—in politics, business, academia, or the mili-
> tary. It's amazing the way some people develop
> during their lives."[2]*

In recent years Gates has become interested in genetics, funding a chair at the University of Washington
for the Human Genome Project. One of his favorite
books is *The Selfish Gene*, a Darwinist approach to

evolution by Oxford zoologist Richard Dawkins. The entertaining little book also is a favorite of Charles Munger, Warren Buffett's longtime business partner.

～

Shortly after Gary Kasparov won his first bout with a chess-playing computer, Gates said:

> *"When the day comes that a computer is chess champion, the milestone won't really be all that meaningful. It shouldn't offend human dignity any more than the realization that a person with binoculars can see distant objects better than a person without binoculars."[3]*

～

At least for now, brains have a distinct advantage over computers:

> *"Playing chess can help teach a person how to apply strategy in other games or situations and possibly even succeed in business, but playing chess can't teach a computer anything."[4]*

～

The day may come, however, when that changes:

> *"I don't think there's anything unique about human intelligence. All the neurons in the brain that make up perceptions and emotions operate in a binary fashion."*

Although human life is carbon based and computers are silicon based, Gates doesn't see a critical distinction:

"Eventually we'll be able to sequence the human genome and replicate how nature did intelligence in a carbon-based system."[5]

~

"Analytically, I would say nature has done a good job making child-raising more pleasure than pain, since that is necessary for a species to survive. But the experience goes beyond the analytic description. Evolution is many orders of magnitude ahead of mankind today in creating a complex system. I don't think it's irreconcilable to say we will understand the human mind some day and explain it in softwarelike terms, and also to say it is a creation that shouldn't be compared to software. Religion has come around to the view that even things that can be explained scientifically can have an underlying purpose that goes beyond science. Even though I am not religious, the amazement and wonder I have about the human mind is closer to religious awe than dispassionate analysis."[6]

GATES'S HEROES

The word "hero," Gates says, may be too strong to describe the people he looked up to and even emulated as a young man. As a child he enjoyed biographies and read about everyone from Newton to Napoleon.

~

Gates was inspired to purchase one of Leonardo da Vinci's 21 surviving notebooks, the Codex Leister, because he has admired the sixteenth century Italian since Gates was ten years old:

> *"Leonardo was one of the most amazing people who ever lived. He was a genius in more fields than any scientist of any age, and an astonishing painter and sculptor."*[7]

The various notebooks, which were compiled in Florence and Milan from 1506 to 1510, predict the invention of helicopters, submarines, and other modern devices. Gates has read part of his notebook in translation; in it da Vinci speculates on hydraulics, cosmology, astronomy, geology, and other topics. Gates says he is sorry that by winning the notebook at an auction for a bid of $30.8 million he upset the Italian people, who hoped that the notebook would return to Italy.

> *"But Leonardo was more than just an Italian, and this notebook is part of the intellectual and cultural heritage of the entire world. It should be shared with the world."*[8]

Gates said he would not exploit the manuscript for commercial purposes but expects to lend it to museums everywhere, starting with a year's stint in an Italian museum.

NOTE: Gates's Corbis Corp. in 1996 published a CD-ROM on Leonardo da Vinci with the Codex as the centerpiece. The CD-ROM's producer says, however, that the CD images were not taken from the actual manuscript. Instead, they were scanned from photographs taken by Seth Joel in 1980 after industrialist Armand Hammer bought the Codex for $5.6 million.[9] The CD-ROM, incidentally, was not a commercial success.

~

Among Gates's more recent heroes are former South African President Nelson Mandela, professional golfer Tiger Woods, and the late Nobel Prize–winning physicist Richard Feynman.

Gates heard Mandela speak shortly after his release from 27 years' imprisonment by the South African apartheid government:

> *"While listening to him talk about the course he charted upon his release, I realized he was totally thoughtful and rational about the importance of putting the past behind him. I kept thinking, 'wait a minute! Where's the emotion? Where's the bitterness here?'*
>
> *"Mandela spoke about how he followed his head, not his heart, because he knew his heart wasn't the way forward. What strength!"*[10]

~

Gates admires Tiger Woods because, at a tender age, he defined a new level of excellence in his field.

~

To his regret, he never met the great Caltech physicist Richard Feynman. Gates says that no sooner had he decided to try to meet Feynman, he picked up *The New York Times* and read that Feynman had died. Feynman, says Gates, was an independent thinker and gifted teacher who pushed himself to understand new things.

"His book, *Surely You're Joking, Mr. Feynman*, is a favorite of mine. I have videotapes of physics lectures Feynman gave at Cornell decades ago. They are the best lectures I've seen on any subject. He shared his enthusiasm and clarity energetically and persuasively."[11]

~

Among the business leaders he admires most, Gates lists Warren Buffett; Jack Welch, Chairman of General Electric; Eckhard Pfeiffer of Compaq; and Andy Grove of Intel.

Gates says he admires Grove because of his ability to see the need for change and adapt his company to new challenges. In 1971 a Japanese customer asked Intel to design memory chips for five new models of desktop calculators. Doing things the old way, Intel would have had to develop 12 different special-purpose chips and face complex manufacturing problems. Instead, Intel developed a general-purpose logic chip that used software to achieve different tasks. This was the beginning of the microprocessor industry.

> *"It was a gutsy and brilliant decision, a real act of leadership by Grove and his colleagues. Today Intel is the king of microprocessors and one of the world's most valuable companies."*[12]

~

Henry Ford, the legendary founder of Ford Motors and inventor of the assembly line, is *not* one of Gates's heroes. Because the motor company was still young when Ford let it fall behind General Motors, Ford remained second in the market for years. Ford's story taught Gates that it's one thing to succeed and another to hold on to success.

~

John Mariotti, head of the consulting firm The Enterprise Group, says Gates is not yet a hero, but could become one: "Bill Gates is young enough to be a real role model for the next generation. So far he has only been 'exposed' as brilliant, tough, visionary, and hugely successful."[13]

~

Yet Gates *has* been a role model an entire generation of programmers and hackers. Many emulate his look and mannerisms. A *Time* magazine reader thinks that more than just nerdy kids admire Gates. "America has a hero in Bill Gates. He's everything we all want to be—smart, creative, dedicated, energetic," wrote Sharon Mirtaheri of Germantown, Maryland.[14]

GATES AND GOD

Gates often is asked about his religious beliefs, practices, and opinions about God. Although he attended church as a youngster, he hasn't placed churchgoing high on his list of needs:

"Just in terms of allocation of time resources, religion is not very efficient. There's a lot more I could be doing on a Sunday morning."[15]

~

Though he is not a regular church-goer, Gates says he sometimes reads the Bible when he's in a hotel room and there's nothing else to read. So does he believe there is a God?

"It's possible, you can never know that the universe exists only for me. If so, it's sure going well for me, I must admit."

The reporter pressed on, asking if there wasn't something special, even divine, about the human soul. Gates began to rock back and forth, a habit he's had since infancy:

"I don't have any evidence on that. I don't have any evidence on that."[16]

~

Gates apparently thinks there is credence to the chaos theory. When asked if his great success indicated that he'd been lucky, he said: "No, my success just proves that life is chaotic. . . . Some butterfly did the right thing for me."[17]

~

Whether he believes in God or not, Gates told Barbara Walters:

"I'm a big believer in religious values."[18]

⌇

If jokes circulating on the Internet are any indication, God and Gates speak often to one another:

Bill Clinton, Al Gore, and Bill Gates were in an airplane crash. They were all swept up to heaven and placed before God's great white throne. God looked down and addressed Gore first. "Al, what do you believe in?" "If any more freon is used," Al replied, "the earth will become a greenhouse and everyone will die." God smiled and said, "Come and sit at my left."

God then addressed Clinton. "Bill, what do you believe in?" Clinton replied, "I believe in feeling people's pain." God smiled and said, "Come and sit at my right."

God then addressed Bill Gates. "Bill, what do you believe?" Gates smiled and said, "I believe you're in my chair."

⌇

God always gets the last laugh:

Bill Gates dies and finds himself being sized up by God.

"Well, Bill, I'm really confused on this call. I'm not sure whether to send you to heaven or hell. After all, you helped society enormously by putting a computer in almost every home in America, yet you also created that ghastly Windows 95. I'm going to do something I've never done before. I'm going to let you decide where you want to go.

Bill replied, "Well, what's the difference between the two?"

God said, "I will let you visit both places briefly, to see if it helps your decision."

So Bill went to hell first. It was beautiful—a clean, sandy beach with blue water and beautiful women frolicking in the surf. The sun was shining and the temperature was perfect.

"This is great," said Bill. "If this is hell, I want to see heaven."

"Fine," said God, and off they went. Heaven was high in the clouds. Angels drifted about playing harps and singing. It was nice but not exciting.

Bill pondered for a moment. "Hmmm. I think I prefer hell," he told God.

In the blink of an eye it was done.

Two weeks later God checked in on Gates to see how he was doing. When God arrived, he found Bill shackled to a wall, screaming among hot flames in dark caves, being burned and tortured by demons.

"How's it going?" asked God.

Bill screamed in anguish, "This is awful. This is nothing like the hell I visited two weeks ago. I can't believe it. What happened to that other place, with the beaches and sunshine and beautiful women?"

"Oh," God said. "That was Hell 3.1. This is Hell 95."

~

But even with God, Gates is Gates:

Bill Clinton, Boris Yeltsin, and Bill Gates were called in by God. God told them he was very unhappy about what was going on in this world. Since things were so bad, he was destroying the earth in three days. They were each allowed to return to their homes and businesses to tell friends and colleagues what was happening.

Bill Clinton called his staff together. "I have good news and bad news for you. First the good news . . . there is a God. The bad news is that he's destroying the earth in three days."

Boris Yeltsin went back and told his people: "I have bad news and more bad news. The first is . . . there is a God. The second is that he is destroying the earth in three days."

Bill Gates returned and told his staff: "I have good news and good news. First . . . God thinks I am one of the three most important people in the world. Second . . . you don't have to fix the bugs in Windows 95."

~

THE BOTTOM LINE

GATES'S PERSONAL PLANS
FOR THE FUTURE

" . . . *the future is what matters, which is why I don't look back too often.*"[1]

∿

Gates's partner, Paul Allen, left Microsoft and launched a business life elsewhere. What would happen to Microsoft if Gates turned his attention away from the company? Stop worrying. Gates likes the job, much of his wealth is tied up in Microsoft, and he views the transition to a new CEO as a risky time for any business:

> "*I'm a younger CEO than you'll find in most companies and more committed to my job than most. Nobody is going to get me interested in some other job or activity, so it's very unlikely that we'd face that challenge.*"[2]

∿

"I have the freedom to do whatever I want. We have this challenge of playing a leadership role in the information age. We're very early in that. It's the only industry I think that's more interesting than biotech. Maybe ten years from now we'll be far enough along, and I'll put my head up and look around."[3]

~

Gates is realistic about the future of his company:

"Microsoft won't be immortal. All companies fail. It's just a question of when. My goal is to keep my company vital as long as possible, of course."[4]

~

Gates expects to take an active role in Microsoft at least until the year 2005, according to a 1995 *Time* magazine interview:

Gates: I have a will written that, you know, talks about how the company should be run and who should vote my shares. There's nobody designated as my successor.

Time: How long do you plan to run Microsoft?

Gates: Well, I'm 39, and my response to that question has always been that for the next decade I plan on playing pretty much the role I am today.

Time: You always answer one decade?

Gates: Yeah, that's as far ahead as I can see.[5]

NOTE: Since then Gates has said that Steve Ballmer will run the company in the event that he himself cannot.

~

"I can't think of being 60 and running the company. By then I will pick a new CEO."[6]

~

Gates says he believes his years in the computer business have been the most fun anyone could ever have:

"I've had to learn a lot. I've had challenges. You can pick any year and I can tell you what the crisis that year was, you know, was it the OS/2 crisis or the Unix crisis. These crises are behind us. We've always got new ones that come in, but I can say with a great deal of confidence that the next 20 years are going to be even more interesting and there will be a lot more to learn that will be even better than what's come before."[7]

~

"Even after 20 years, I still think I have the best job in the world. I am constantly challenged by the technology, the speed with which the business changes and by the incredibly smart people I work with inside Microsoft and elsewhere. There are so many people I've had fun working with it's hard to pick just a few, but Paul Allen, obviously, was a great guy to start Microsoft with, and Steve Ballmer has been my best friend for many, many years. A lot of people like the idea of having a job that helps change the world in a positive way, and I have that satisfaction."[8]

~

HAS IT BEEN WORTH IT?

"It's like walking the Vatican with the Pope," observed NBC newscaster Tom Brokaw, after strolling with Gates through the Las Vegas Comdex computer show.[9]

~

Gates has achieved fame and nearly unimaginable wealth, but even he doesn't have it all:

"I never got to spend a decade thinking about economics. I never got to be a biochemist. I never scored 72 in a game of golf and it's unlikely I ever will, though I hold out faint hope (my best score is 87)."[10]

~

Gates says he's had many personal failures:

"When I was young I wanted to be the world's best chess player and, of course, I didn't succeed. I wanted to be the world's best Go player, too. I wanted to keep IBM in a happy partnership with Microsoft, and that didn't work out either. There are people I wanted to hire whom I couldn't. So I've had plenty of disappointments."[11]

~

Gates says that if he were not working in the field of information technology, he might choose biotechnology. Genome research, the study of the vast road map of human genetic makeup, especially interests him. He helped finance a molecular biology program at the University of Washington and sits on the boards of

227

ICOS Corp. and Darwin Molecular Corp., both small, privately held biotech companies:

> *"A disease for which there is no effective therapy is an unsolved mystery."*[12]

~

As fascinating as he finds genetics, Gates doesn't seriously wish he'd taken a different career path:

> *"I don't waste much time ruing the past. I made my decision, and the way to do it best is, once you make it, you just don't waver at all. You don't think, gosh, what a doctor I would've been, what a tennis player, playboy, poker player I couldn't been. Being hardcore and forward looking about what you do is a necessary element of doing it well."*[13]

~

Even so, Gates and Paul Allen enjoy reminiscing:

> *"We like to talk about how the fantasies we had as kids and the neat things we dreamed about [that] actually came true."*[14]

~

In fact, Gates is pretty satisfied with life in general:

> *"Science fiction suggests that someday hundreds of people will fill a huge starship and spend generations traveling to a star. For example, the great grandchildren of the original voyagers might complete the trip.*

"*Maybe so, but I'm not getting on that ship! I'm sticking here. We have lakes. We have rivers. We have mountains. Earth is amazing compared to what's available in the surrounding few light-years.*"[15]

~

"*It's a great time to be alive.*"[16]

THE BILL GATES
TIME LINE

1955: William Henry Gates III was born to William H. and Mary Maxwell Gates on October 28 shortly after 9 P.M. in Seattle, Washington.

1967: Gates is enrolled in the small and exclusive Lakeside School in Seattle, which is known for its exceptional students.

1968: Lakeside School Mother's Club gave the school a Digital training terminal, linked by telephone to a computer at a local computing company.

1972: Gates served as a congressional page during the summer.

1973: Gates graduated from Lakeside High School and enrolled in Harvard University, where he majored in pre-law.

1974: The MITS Altair kit computer, mostly for electronic hobbyists, went on sale for $397.

1975: In a frantic eight-week rush, using BASIC, Bill Gates and school pal Paul G. Allen wrote the first software language for a personal computer.

April 14: Gates and Allen established Micro-Soft as a partnership and began business in Albuquerque, New Mexico.

1976: Gates wrote the now-famous, scathing "Open Letter to Hobbyists," accusing them of pirating software and therefore retarding software development. For the first time, concern over software piracy became a public issue.

1977: Following a painful lawsuit, Micro-Soft was released from its contract with MITS and owned its BASIC outright.

Gates met Kuzuhiko Nishi, who developed Microsoft markets in Japan.

Microsoft shipped its second software language for PC, this one written in FORTRAN.

1978: Microsoft established an international sales office in Japan.

1979: In January, Gates and Allen moved Microsoft—now without a hyphen—to Bellevue, Washington.

1980: Microsoft acquired a small operating system and developed MS-DOS for use on IBM's first personal computer. The MS-DOS operating system was the key to Microsoft's phenomenal success.

Steve Ballmer, Gates's friend from Harvard, became personal assistant to the president, marking Microsoft's transition from a start-up company to a professionally managed corporation.

Microsoft licensed the UNIX operating system.

1981: *June 25*: Microsoft was incorporated with Gates as chairman and CEO. Steve Ballmer was executive vice president of sales and support; Bob Herbold, executive vice president and chief operating officer.

August 12: IBM introduced the personal computer, to be known as the PC, which used Microsoft's 16-bit operating system, MS-DOS Version 1.0.

Gates and Allen sold 6.2 percent of Microsoft to a venture capital company, Technology Venture Investors, of Menlo Park, California, as a preliminary to going public.

1982: Paul Allen was diagnosed with Hodgkin's disease, a form of cancer. He left the company but returned a year later when the disease went into remission.

1983: *Time* magazine named the personal computer the "Machine of the Year," displacing the traditional "Man of the Year."

1984: Apple Computer introduced the Macintosh, the first serious competitor to the IBM PC for the business-computer user.

1985: Microsoft and IBM cooperated on the powerful OS/2 operating system, intended to replace MS-DOS.

Microsoft introduced Windows 1.0, but it was slow and unpopular.

Gates delivered his first keynote address at Comdex.

1986: Gates became a billionaire, at 31 years of age, the youngest person to ever to do so.

March 13: Microsoft became a public company, with initial shares priced at $21. The shares first traded at 9:35 A.M. at $25.75, peaked at $29.25, and closed the day at $27.75. Microsoft raised $61 million in the public offering.

Microsoft's 1,200 employees moved to a new 29-acre office campus in Redmond, Washington. By 1998 there were 49 buildings and nearly 15,000 of Microsoft's 24,000 employees worked there.

Compaq Computer Corp. introduced its first desktop PC, a serious contender to the IBM PC.

Gates and Allen gave Lakeside School $2.2 million to build a science and math center.

1987: Microsoft and IBM introduced OS/2. The system did not live up to expectations that it would set the new standard. Gates was accused of neglecting OS/2 in favor of Microsoft's own Windows.

Microsoft beat out Lotus Development to become the largest software company in the world, based on sales.

1990: *May 22*: In a whirl of publicity, Windows 3.0 was introduced. The program was an instant success, selling 1 million copies in the first four months. Microsoft cemented its position as the leading vendor of operating systems.

Microsoft's net revenues topped $1 billion for the first time.

1991: Apple Computer filed a copyright suit against Microsoft, alleging that Windows violated Apple's copyrights on the Macintosh operating system.

The Federal Trade Commission began investigating Microsoft for anticompetitive practices.

1992: On the first trading day of the year, Microsoft's stock closed at $114 per share. (The shares split three for two several months earlier.) For the first time, Bill Gates was the wealthiest person in America, at least on paper.

Bill Gates received the National Medal of Technology from President George Bush.

1994: Gates and Melinda French were married on New Year's Day in Hawaii.

With a net worth of $9.35 billion, Bill Gates, 38, toppled Warren Buffett, 64, from the title of wealthiest American.

Microsoft and the Justice Department reached a settlement agreement over allegations of unfair competition. The Justice Department later charged Microsoft with breaching the agreement.

Mary Gates died of breast cancer.

1995: Gates became the world's richest private individual with a net worth of $12.9 billion. Warren Buffett, chairman of Berkshire Hathaway was number two with $12.7 billion.

Gates was voted "most respected CEO" in *Industry Week* survey. He beat GE's Jack Welch by one vote.

August 24: With great fanfare, Windows 95 was introduced.

December 7: Gates announced Microsoft's push into the Internet business, a move that eventually led to new antitrust actions from the government.

1996: Warren Buffett tipped Gates from number one on the "world's wealthiest" list. Buffett was worth $17 billion. Gates's shares in Microsoft made his worth a measly $14.3 billion.

Jennifer Katharine Gates was born on April 26.

1997: *May 28*: Gates sold 340,000 shares of Microsoft and collected $39,142,500.

July: Microsoft invested $1 billion in cable company Comcast.

1998: Bill, Melinda, and Jennifer Gates moved into their multimillion-dollar Medina, Washington, estate, though construction continued.

Gates and Allen filed with the Securities and Exchange Commission to sell a total of $570 million in stock. According to a Microsoft spokesperson, Gates has a program to sell stock at regular intervals to diversify his portfolio.

Steve Ballmer was named president of Microsoft. Gates remained CEO.

ENDNOTES

Preface

1. "The Most Intriguing People of 1983," *People*, December 26, 1983.

2. Rich Karlgaard, "Silicon Valley's Politics of Envy," *The Wall Street Journal*, October 20, 1997, p. A20.

3. Bill Gates Joke Page, http://www.vantek.net/pages/hydra/gates/bgip.html.

4. Business Wire, November 14, 1997.

5. Adapted from G. Pascal Zachary, *Show Stopper!: The Breakneck Race to Create Windows NT and the Next Generation at Microsoft* (New York: The Free Press, 1994). Reprinted in *Computerworld*, October 17, 1994.

6. Nathan Myhrvold, "The Dawn of Technomania," *The New Yorker*, October 20, 1997, p. 236.

7. Richard Karlgaard, "Silicon Valley's Politics of Envy," *The Wall Street Journal*, October 20, 1997, p. A20.

8. Elise O'Shaughnessy, "The New Establishment," *Vanity Fair*, October 1994, p. 214.

9. Stephanie Gruner, "The Most-Admired Entrepreneurs," *Inc.*, September 1997, p. 109.

10. David Bank and John R. Wilke, "Microsoft and Justice End a Skirmish, Yet War Could Escalate," *The Wall Street Journal*, January 23, 1998, p. 1.

11. John W. Huey, Jr., "Yes, It's Gates—Again," *Fortune*, May 26, 1997, p. 10.

Growing Up Gates

1. Bill Gates, Column, New York Times Syndicate, May 6, 1997.

2. "The Gates Operating System," *Time*, January 13, 1997.

3. Bill Gates, Column, New York Times Syndicate, August 26, 1997.

4. James Wallace and Jim Erickson, *Hard Drive* (New York: John Wiley & Sons, Inc., 1992), p. 7.

5. Bill Gates, e-mail interview with author, April 30, 1998.

6. Bill Gates, Column, New York Times Syndicate, June 4, 1996.

7. Richard Dean Anderson, "Superstar Scouts," *Boys Life*, June 1994, p. 29.

8. David Rensin, "The Bill Gates Interview," *Playboy*, December 8, 1994.

9. Chelsea J. Carter, "Personal Computer Was Doctor's Baby," *The San Diego Union Tribune*, December 1, 1997, p. D3.

10. John Seabrook, "E-Mail from Bill," *The New Yorker*, January 10, 1994, p. 58.

11. O. Casey Corr, "Melinda French Gates: A Microsoft Mystery," *The Seattle Times*, June 4, 1995, p. C1.

12. "Diagnosing Bill Gates," *Time*, January 24, 1994, p. 25.

13. Richard Brandt, "The Billion-Dollar Whiz Kid," *Business Week*, April 13, 1987.

14. Brent Schendler, "Bill & Paul Talk," *Fortune*, October 2, 1995, p. 69.

15. Bill Gates, Speech, Lakeside High School, 1995.

16. Lisa Russell, "Quote of the Week," *People*, September 11, 1995.

17. William Plummer, "Paul Allen," *People*, June 19, 1995, p. 105.

18. Susan Lammers, *Programmers at Work* (Redmond, Wash.: Microsoft Press, 1986), p. 76.

19. Michael Moritz, "A Hardcore Technoid," *Time*, April 16, 1984, p. 63.

20. Daniel Ichbiah and Susan L. Knepper, *The Making of Microsoft* (Rocklin, Calif.: Prima Publishing, 1991), p. 7.

21. Bill Gates, Column, New York Times Syndicate, November 19, 1996.

22. Ibid.

23. Current Biography Year Book (New York: W. H. Wilson, 1991), p. 238.

24. Paul Frieberger and Michael Swaine, *Fire in the Valley* (Berkeley, Calif.: Osborne/McGraw-Hill, 1984), p. 24.

25. Moritz, "A Hardcore Technoid."

26. Bill Gates, Speech, Cambridge University, Cambridge, England, October 7, 1997.

27. Douglas Bartholomew, "Bill Gates Envisions the Enterprise," *Industry Week*, December 16, 1996, p. 9.

28. Bill Gates, Speech, Kellogg Technology Series, Evanston, Illinois, April 29, 1997.

29. Robert Slater, *Portraits in Silicon* (Cambridge, Mass: The MIT Press, 1987), p. 264.

30. Gates, Speech, Cambridge University.

31. "Dropping Out of Harvard Pays Off for a Computer Whiz Kid Who's Making Hard Cash From Software," *People*, December 26, 1983, p. 37.

32. Lammers, *Programmers at Work*.

33. Dr. Terry Macaluso's introduction of Bill Gates when Gates spoke at Lakeside High School, 1995.

Heading Off on the Conventional Road

1. Jeffrey Young, "The George S. Patton of Software," *Forbes*, January 27, 1997, p. 86.

2. John Seabrook, "E-Mail from Bill," *The New Yorker*, January 10, 1994, p. 58.

3. Michael W. Miller, "How Two Computer Nuts Transformed Industry Before Messy Breakup," *The Wall Street Journal*, August 27, 1986.

4. Bill Gates, Keynote speech, Stanford University, Palo Alto, California, January 27, 1998.

5. Bill Gates, Column, New York Times Syndicate, May 8, 1996.

6. Ibid.

7. Michael Maritz, "A Hardcore Technoid," *Time*, April 16, 1984, p. 63.

8. Robert Slater, *Portraits in Silicon* (Cambridge, Mass: The MIT Press, 1987), p. 265.

9. Ibid.

10. "Interview: Gordon Moore, Intel," *PC Magazine*, March 25, 1997.

11. Bill Gates, Speech sponsored by the City of Chicago and the Chicago Public Library, March 19, 1996.

12. "Dropping Out of Harvard Pays Off for a Computer Whiz Kid Who's Making Hard Cash from Software," *People*, December 26, 1983, p. 37.

13. Bill Gates, Speech, Developer Days, Seattle, Washington, March 18, 1997.

14. Bill Gates, Speech, Tech Ed '96.

Back on the High-Tech Highway

1. Ed Zuckerman, *People*, August 20, 1990.

2. James Wallace and Jim Erickson, *Hard Drive* (New York: John Wiley & Sons, 1992), p. 76.

3. Ibid.

4. Doug Bartholomew, "Bill Gates Envisions the Enterprise," *Industry Week*, December 16, 1996, p. 9.

5. Bill Gates, Column, New York Times Syndicate, June 4, 1996.

6. Susan Lammers, *Programmers at Work* (Redmond, Wash.: Microsoft Press, 1986), p. 72.

7. Bill Gates, Column, New York Times Syndicate, December 17, 1996.

8. Bill Gates, Column, New York Times Syndicate, March 14, 1995.

9. "Just Two Billionaire Buddies Sitting Around on a Sunday Afternoon Reminiscing about Inventing the Most Important Software Ever," Press Release, *Time Inc.*, September 12, 1997.

10. Brent Schlender, "Bill & Paul Talk," *Fortune*, October 2, 1996, p. 68.

11. Daniel Ichbiah and Susan L. Knepper, *The Making of Microsoft* (Rocklin, Calif.: Prima Publishing, 1991), p. 45.

12. Wallace and Erickson, *Hard Drive*, p. 117.

13. David Bank and John R. Wilke, "Microsoft and Justice End a Skirmish, Yet War Could Escalate," *The Wall Street Journal*, January 23, 1998, p. 1.

14. "Bill Gates," *Money Magazine*, July 1986.

15. James Chposky and Ted Leonsis, *Blue Magic* (New York: Facts On File, 1988), p. 45.

16. Paul Carroll, *Big Blues: The Unmaking of IBM* (New York: Crown Publishers, 1993), p. 34.

17. "How We Did It," *Newsweek*, June 23, 1997, p. 78.

18. Andrew Shulman, "The United States Versus Bill Gates," *Newsweek*, July 11, 1994, p. 43.

19. Ichbiah and Knepper, *The Making of Microsoft*, p. 226.

20. Bill Gates, "Watching His Windows," *Forbes ASAP*, December 1, 1997, p. 142.

21. Bill Gates, e-mail interview with author, April 30, 1998.

22. Stanley W. Angrist, "Big Is Beautiful," *The Wall Street Journal*, February 13, 1998, p. A12.

23. Simon Walch, "X-Ray," America Online, January 26, 1998.

24. Bill Gates, Column, New York Times Syndicate, March 12, 1997.

25. Bill Gates, e-mail interview with author, April 30, 1998.

26. "Money & Markets," *Fortune*, July 21, 1986, p. 24.

27. Randall E. Stross, *The Microsoft Way: The Real Story of How the Company Outsmarts Its Competitors* (Reading, Mass.: Addison-Wesley, 1996), p. 24.

28. Bill Gates, e-mail interview with author, April 30, 1998.

29. David Kirkpatrick, "How Bill Gates Sees the Future," *Fortune*, June 28, 1993.

The Gatesian Management Style

1. "Bill Gates," *Forbes*, December 7, 1992.

2. G. Pascal Zachary, *Show Stopper!: The Breakneck Race to Create Windows NT and the Next Generation at Microsoft* (New York: The Free Press, 1994), p. 30.

3. Bill Gates, with Nathan Myhrvold and Bill Rinearson, *The Road Ahead* (New York: Penguin Books, 1995), p. 208.

4. "The Gates Operating System," *Time*, January 13, 1997.

5. Michael Meyer, "Culture Club," *Newsweek*, July 11, 1994, p. 38.

6 Kara Swisher, "A Web Pioneer Does a Delicate Dance with Microsoft," *The Wall Street Journal*, February 12, 1998.

7. Bill Gates, "Ask Bill," New York Times Syndicate, April 11, 1995.

8. Randall E. Stross, *The Microsoft Way: The Real Story of How the Company Outsmarts Its Competitors* (Reading, Mass.: Addison-Wesley, 1996) p. 3.

9. Lynn Povich, "On-line with Bill Gates," *Working Woman*, January 1996, p. 41.

10. Leslie Helm, "Microsoft Testing Limits on Temp Worker Use," *Los Angeles Times*, December 7, 1997.

11. Ibid.

12. Jeffrey Young, "The Field Marshals," *Forbes*, January 27, 1997, p. 90.

13. William Plummer, "Paul Allen," *People*, June 19, 1995, p. 105.

14. ASAP Technology 100, www.Forbes.com

15. "Just Two Billionaire Buddies Sitting Around on a Sunday Afternoon Reminiscing About Inventing the Most Important Software Ever," Press Release, *Time Inc.*, September 12, 1997.

16. Tania Chau, John Goldstein, Anita Hamilton, and Melissa Scram, "Cyber Elite Technology Has Ushered in a New Ruling Class," *Time*, October 1, 1997.

17. Jeffrey Young, "The George S. Patton of Software," *Forbes*, January 27, 1997, p. 86.

18. Ibid.

19. "Of Bytes and Bites," *The New Yorker*, December 4, 1995, p. 38.

20. Randall E. Stross, "Mr. Gates Builds His Brain Trust," *Fortune*, December 8, 1997.

21. Ibid.

22. Julie Pitta, "Microsoft's Other Boy Genius," *Forbes*, August 2, 1993, p. 122.

23. Daniel Ichbiah and Susan L. Knepper, *The Making of Microsoft* (Rocklin, Calif.: Prima Publishing, 1991), p. 56.

24. Michael W. Miller, "How Two Computer Nuts Transformed Industry Before Messy Breakup," *The Wall Street Journal*, August 27, 1986, p. A1.

25. Ibid.

26. Ibid and James Chposky and Ted Leonsis, *Blue Magic* (New York: Facts on File Publications, 1988), p. 51.

27. "Tycoon," NBC Special with Tom Brokaw, May 28, 1995.

28. Bill Gates, e-mail interview with author, April 30, 1998.

29. Bill Gates, Column, New York Times Syndicate, July 31, 1996.

30. Pitta, "Microsoft's Other Boy Genius."

31. Bill Gates, "Companies Need Digital Nervous Systems," New York Times Special Features, May 21, 1997.

32. Zachary, *Show Stopper!*, p. 250.

33. Martin Wolk, "Dateline Seattle," Reuters, October 21, 1997.

34. Bill Gates, "Leaders Must be Candid, Consistent," New York Times Syndicate, September 12, 1996.

35. Ibid.

36. Zachary, *Show Stopper!*, p. 284.

37. Bill Gates, Column, New York Times Syndicate, March 11, 1998.

38. David Rensin, "The Bill Gates Interview," *Playboy*, December 8, 1994.

39. Andrew Shulman, "The United States Versus Bill Gates," *Newsweek*, July 11, 1994, p. 43.

40. Fred Moody, "The Life of Bill," Special to ABCNEWS.com, January 30, 1998.

41. Stephen Manes and Paul Andrews, *Gates: How Microsoft's Mogul Reinvented an Industry, and Made Himself the Richest Man in America* (New York: Doubleday, 1993), p. 442.

42. Pitta, "Microsoft's Other Boy Genius."

43. Brent Schlender, "A Conversation with the Lords of Wintel," *Fortune*, July 8, 1996, p. 42.

44. "Vanity Fair's Second Annual Top 50 Leaders of the Information Age," *Vanity Fair*, October 1996, p. 100.

45. Chris Peters, *Shipping Software*, Microsoft video, 1990.

46. "Technology," Bill Gates, *The Costco Connection*, November 1997, p. 19.

47. Steven Levy, "Gates, Face to Face," *Newsweek*, December 2, 1996, p. 62.
48. Bill Gates, "Office 'Retreat' Should Be Work," New York Times Special Features, October 9, 1996.
49. Bill Gates, "Davos Was No Boondoggle," New York Times Special Features, February 25, 1997.
50. Bill Gates, "Ask Bill Gates," New York Times Syndicate, August 29, 1995.
51. Alan Deutschman, "Bill Gates' Next Challenge," *Fortune*, December 28, 1992.
52. Daniel Ichbiah and Susan L. Knepper, *The Making of Microsoft* (Rocklin, Calif.: Prima Publishing, 1991), p. 40.
53. Bill Gates, Column, New York Times Syndicate, February 12, 1996.
54. Michael Moritz, "A Hardcore Technoid," *Time*, April 16, 1984, p. 63.
55. Bill Gates, Column, New York Times Syndicate," September 25, 1997.
56. Ibid.
57. Bill Gates, Column, The New York Times Syndicate, March 14, 1995.
58. Michael A. Cusumano and Richard W. Selby, *Microsoft Secrets* (New York: The Free Press, 1995), p. 28.
59. Ichbiah and Knepper, *The Making of Microsoft*, p. 40.
60. Manes and Andrews, *Gates*, p. 308.
61. Ibid., p. 406.
62. Steven Levy, "Bill's New Vision," *Newsweek*, November 27, 1995.
63. Bill Gates, Speech, annual meeting of the American Association for the Advancement of Science, Seattle, Washington, February 17, 1997.

The Microsoft Business Model

1. George Taninecz, "Gates Wins Respect," *Industry Week*, November 20, 1995, p. 12.
2. Michael A. Cusamano and Richard W. Selby, Microsoft Secrets (New York: The Free Press, 1995), pp. 25–26.
3. Bill Gates, "Ask Bill," New York Times Syndicate, January 14, 1997.
4. "What Does Bill Want," *Forbes*, January 27, 1997, p. 102.
5. John Emmerling, "Gates-ian Ideas Work in Ad Biz," *Advertising Age*, September 23, 1996, p. 31.
6. Donald Spenser, *Great Men and Women of Computing* (Ormond Beach, Fl.: Camelot Publishing Co., 1996), p. 162.
7. Susan Lammers, *Programmers at Work* (Redmond, Wash.: Microsoft Press, 1986) p. 83.
8. George Taninecz, "Gates Wins Respect," *Industry Week*, November 20, 1995, p. 12.
9. Bill Gates, "What Makes a Good Manager," New York Times Special Features, October 8, 1997.
10. John Emmerling, "Gates-ian Ideas Work in Ad Biz," *Advertising Age*, September 23, 1996, p. 31.
11. Philip Elmer-DeWitt, "Mine, All Mine," *Time*, June 5, 1995.

12. Gates, "What Makes a Good Manager."

13. Bill Gates, Speech, Windows TCO Summit, Tokyo, Japan, June 19, 1997.

14. Taninecz, "Gates Wins Respect," p. 17.

15. Cusumano and Selby, *Microsoft Secrets.*

16. Bill Gates, "Customer-Driven Firms Need Feedback," New York Times Special Features, August 13, 1996.

17. Michael Meyer, "Culture Club," *Newsweek*, July 11, 1994, p. 38.

18. Bill Gates, Speech, Microsoft Tech Ed '97, Orlando, Florida, May 5, 1997.

19. Bill Gates, Speech, WinHEC 97, San Francisco, California, April 8, 1997.

20. Elmer-DeWitt, "Mine, All Mine."

21. William J. Cook, "The New Rockefeller," *U.S. News & World Report*, February 15, 1993, p. 64.

22. Ibid.

23. Brent Schlender, "Smart Managing: Microsoft, First America, Now the World," *Fortune*, August 18, 1997.

24. Bill Gates, Speech, Analyst Summit 97, Seattle, Washington, July 24, 1997.

25. Gates, speech, Windows TCO Summit, Tokyo.

26. Schlender, "Smart Managing."

27. Schlender, "On the Road with Chairman Bill," *Fortune*, May 26, 1997.

28. "Bill Gates Goes A-Wooing to India," Newsbytes News Network, March 6, 1997.

29. Bill Gates, Column, New York Times Syndicate, April 8, 1997.

30. "Bill's Trip: Europe," Microsoft Web site.

31. Bill Gates, "Laying a Foundation for Human History," Column, Microsoft Web site, November 5, 1997.

32. Kathy Rebello, "Bill's Quiet Shopping Spree," *Business Week*, January 13, 1997.

33. Bill Gates, Speech, Seybold 97, San Francisco, California, October 1, 1997.

34. Ibid.

35. John R. Wilke and David Bank, "Microsoft's Chief Concedes Hardball Tactics," *The Wall Street Journal*, March 4, 1998, p. B1.

36. Steven Hamm, "Microsoft Refines Its Net Game," *Business Week*, September 8, 1997.

37. "The Smithsonian Time Machine," *Smithsonian*, August, 1996.

38. Kathy Rebello, "Bill's Quiet Shopping Spree," *Business Week*, January 13, 1997.

39. Bill Gates, Speech, Stanford University, Palo Alto, California, January 27, 1998.

40. Bill Gates, Speech, Newspaper Association of America Publishers' Convention, Chicago, Illinois, April 29, 1997.

41. Bill Gates, Speech, Microsoft Corporation Empowerment 2001, Seattle, Washington, February 9, 1998.

42. Bill Gates, Speech, Microsoft Corporation Empowerment 2001, Seattle, Washington, February 9, 1998.

43. Bill Gates, "My Vision for the Future," *Net News*, August 10, 1997.

44. Gates, speech, annual AAAS meeting.

45. Bill Gates, Column, New York Times Syndicate, December 20, 1995.

The Computer Wars

1. G. Pascal Zachary, *Show Stopper! The Breakneck Race to Create Windows NT and the Next Generation at Microsoft* (New York: The Free Press, 1994), p. 26.

2. Steve Hamm, "Microsoft to Pirates: Pretty Please?" *Business Week*, September 22, 1997.

3. Reuters, Seattle, November 20, 1997.

4. Jonathan Friedland, "Software Makers Assail Argentine Piracy Ruling," *The Wall Street Journal*, February 6, 1998.

5. "Gates: From OS to Internet," *PC Week Online*, May 30, 1996.

6. Randall Stross, "Heaven's Gates," *U.S. News & World Report*, November 25, 1996, p. 61.

7. Dean Katz, Group Public Relations Manager, e-mail to author, June 11, 1998.

8. Kara Swisher, "Oh What a Tangled Web Silicon Valley Moguls Weave," *The Wall Street Journal*, March 5, 1998, p. B6.

9. Alan Deutschman, "Imposter Boy," *GQ*, January 1997, p. 126.

10. Jerry Kaplan, *Start Up: A Silicon Valley Adventure* (New York: Houghton Mifflin, 1994), p. 16.

11. Zachary, *Show Stopper!*, p. 29.

12. Steve Hamm, "Operation Sunblock: Microsoft Goes to War," *Business Week*, October 27, 1997.

13. James Kim, "Networking: On-line Service Will Be Key," *USA Today*, August 24, 1995.

14. Charles Piller, "Sifting Through Myths, Facts about Apple," *Los Angeles Times*, December 29, 1997.

15. David Lawsky, "Gates and Nader Trade Bitter Barbs at 3,000 Miles," Reuters Business Report, November 14, 1997.

16. Ibid.

17. Michael Schroeder and Bryan Gruley, "Dole Is Helping Efforts to Curb Microsoft Plans," *The Wall Street Journal*, December 23, 1997, p. A16.

18. Rich Karlgaard, "Silicon Valley's Politics of Envy," *The Wall Street Journal*, October 20, 1997, p. A20.

19. Martin Wolk, Reuters, November 14, 1997.

20. Ibid.

21. David Bank and Don Clark, "Microsoft Looks at Ways to Soften Image Tarnished by Legal Dispute with U.S.," *The Wall Street Journal*, January 8, 1998, p. B6.

22. Widely quoted.

23. Ray Richmond, "Flood-Gates Worry Top Cable Executives," *Variety*, December 11, 1997.

24. Guy de Jonquieres, "US Top of the Table," *Financial Times*, September 18, 1996.

25. Michael Moeller, "For Sun and Microsoft, a Rocky Road Leads to the Courthouse," *PC Week Online*, October 7, 1997.

26. Sun Microsystems press release, Business Wire, November 24, 1997.

27. Chris Taylor, "Firing Back at Bill," *Time*, December 18, 1997.

28. Mary Jo Foley, "Gates Decries 'Witch Hunt,'" *PC Week Online*, November 14, 1997.

29. "Laugh Lines," *Los Angeles Times*, October 22, 1977.

30. Amy Cortese, "Let It Go, Mr. Gates. You'll Win Anyway," *Business Week*, December 29, 1997.

31. Lisa Bowman, "Gates Gives Critics an 'F,'" *Z Net*, January 28, 1998.

32. "Microsoft Isn't 'Defiant' in Justice Case, Gates Says," *The Wall Street Journal*, January 28, 1998.

33. David Bank and John R. Wilke, "Microsoft and Justice End a Skirmish, Yet War Could Escalate," *The Wall Street Journal*, January 31, 1998.

34. Catherine Yang, "Microsoft Goes Low-Tech in Washington," *Business Week*, December 22, 1997, p. 34.

35. Thomas G. Donlon, "The Pursuit of Power," *Barron's*, March 9, 1998, p. 63.

36. Christopher Barr, "Gates Lashes Out at Press," *CNET News*, January 27, 1998.

37. Reuters, March 3, 1998.

38. David Lawsky, Reuters, March 3, 1998.

39. John Dodge, "Let Be Crystal Clear: I Am Not a 'Microsoft Hater,'" *PC Week*, November 10, 1997.

40. Steven Levy, "Gates, Face to Face," *Newsweek*, December 2, 1996, p. 62.

41. Connie Guglielmo, "Gates Says DOJ, Competitors Want to Cripple Microsoft," *Inter@active Week*, January 28, 1998.

42. David Bank, "Why Software and Antitrust Law Make an Uneasy Mix," *The Wall Street Journal*, October 22, 1997, p. B1.

43. Rob Wells, "Microsoft Chief Denies Monopoly," The Associated Press, March 3, 1998.

44. Bill Gates, Address to Shareholders, Microsoft Corp. Annual Shareholders' Meeting, Seattle, Washington, November 14, 1997.

45. Steward Deck, "Microsoft Strong-Arming Is 'Common Knowledge,' Sun Exec Says," *Computerworld*, October 23, 1997.

46. "In Their Own Words," *The Wall Street Journal*, March 4, 1998, p. B1.

47. Greg's Micro$oft Humor page. Http://www.cs.bgu.ac.il/~pribushg/jokes.html.

48. John R. Wilke and Bryan Gruley, "Is Antitrust Relevant in This Digital Age?" *The Wall Street Journal*, December 22, 1997, p. 1.

49. Charles T. Munger, 39th Annual Meeting, Wesco Financial Corp., Pasadena, California, May 25, 1998.

50. Steve Hamm, "Bill Gates: I'm Humble and Respectful," *Business Week*, February 9, 1998.

51. Dateline Las Vegas, Reuters, November 17, 1997.

52. Jube Shiver, Jr. and Leslie Helm, "U.S., 20 States File Antitrust Lawsuits Against Microsoft," *Los Angeles Times*, May 19, 1998, p. A1.

53. "Dear Prudence," *Slate*, December 20, 1997.

54. "On the Road With Bill Gates," *Forbes ASAP*, February 28, 1994.

55. Jonathan Mandell, "Notebook: Fur and Money Fly as Computer Moguls Collide," *Newsday*, July 20, 1997.

56. Dan Bricklin, "The 20 Most Important People," *Byte*, September 1995, p. 133.

57. Charles H. Ferguson and Charles R. Morris, *Computer Wars: How the West Can Win in a Post-IBM World* (New York: Times Books, 1993), p. 74.

58. Paul Carroll, *Big Blues: The Unmaking of IBM* (New York: Crown Publishers, 1993), p. 103.

59. Bill Gates, with Nathan Myhrvold and Peter Rinearson, *The Road Ahead* (New York: Penguin Books, 1995), p. 319.

60. Jeffrey Young, "The George S. Patton of Software," *Forbes*, January 27, 1997, p. 86.

61. Bill Gates, "Office 'Retreat' Should Be Work," New York Times Special Feature, October 9, 1996.

62. Carroll, *Big Blues:*, p. 118.

63. Ibid, p. 90.

64. Tyler Mathisen, "Microsoft's Bill Gates Sizes Up Five Major Computer Companies," *Money*, August, 1993, p. 48.

65. Bill Gates, e-mail interview with author, April 30, 1998.

66. Bill Gates, Keynote speech, Fall 1995 Comdex, Las Vegas, Nevada.

67. Joshua Quittner, "Kinsley's Moment of Truth," *Time*, January 20, 1997.

68. Transcript of *Eye to Eye* broadcast, May 19, 1994.

69. Richard Brandt and Eric Nee, "Bill Gates—An Interview," *Upside*, April 1996.

70. Stephan Manes and Paul Andrews, *Gates: How Microsoft's Mogul Reinvented an Industry—and Made Himself the Richest Man in America*, (New York: Doubleday, 1993), p. 429.

71. "Microsoft Offers 'Patch' to Ward Off NT Hackers," *The Wall Street Journal*, March 5, 1998, p. A16.

Microsoft Mistakes

1. Michael Meyer, "Culture Club," *Newsweek*, July 11, 1994, p. 38.

2. Bill Gates, Keynote speech, Consumer Electronics Show (CES), Las Vegas, Nevada, January 10, 1998.

3. Brent Schlender, "What Does Bill Gates Want," *Fortune*, January 16, 1995, p. 35.

4. Peter Huber, "Reno Rewrites Your Operating System," *Forbes*, December 1, 1997.

5. Jai Sing and Doug Barney, "Gates Unguarded," *InfoWorld*, November 21, 1994, p. 10.

6. Ibid.

7. Steven Levy, "Microsoft vs. the World," *Newsweek*, March 9, 1998.

8. Bill Gates, "Ask Bill," New York Times Syndicate, November 19, 1996.

9. Bill Gates, Speech, Internet World 1996, April 30, 1996.

10. Bill Gates, "Ask Bill," New York Times Syndicate, June 4, 1997.

11. Levy, "Microsoft vs. the World," *Newsweek*, March 9, 1998.

12. Bill Gates, Speech, Internet Explorer 4.0 Launch, San Francisco, California, September 30, 1997.

13. Bill Gates, Column, New York Times Syndicate, January 14, 1997.

14. Bill Gates, "Ask Bill," New York Times Syndicate, February 12, 1996.

15. Bill Gates, Speech, Learn Education Conference, Seattle, Washington, June 30, 1997.

16. "Microsoft: A Lesson in Management," *Business Week*, July 15, 1996, p. 98.

17. Brent Schlender, "An E-Mail Interview with Bill Gates," *Fortune*, December 11, 1995, p. 134.

18. Steve Hamm, "Gates to CEOs: Buy My Stuff," *ZDNN*, May 9, 1997.

19. David Bank, "How One Sweet Deal Unraveled for Netscape After Microsoft Called," *The Wall Street Journal*, November 13, 1997.

Attack the Future

1. Bill Gates, Column, New York Times Syndicate, August 28, 1996.

2. Charles Arthur, "Apple Computer's Biggest Mistake—and What Might Have Been," *Independent*, November 4, 1997.

3. Lee Gomes, "H-P to Market Its Own Strain of Java," *The Wall Street Journal*, March 20, 1998, p. A3.

4. Steve Hamm, "Operation Sunblock: Microsoft Goes to War," *Business Week*, October 27, 1997.

5. Bill Gates, Interview, Gartner Symposium, Orlando, Florida, October 6, 1997.

6. Bill Gates, Address to shareholders, Microsoft Corp. Annual Shareholder's Meeting, November 14, 1997.

7. Andrew Shulman, "The United States versus Bill Gates," *Newsweek*, July 11, 1994, p. 43.

8. IBM Advertisement, *The Wall Street Journal*, December 22, 2997, p. A7.

9. Richard M. Smith, "Bill's Excellent Future," *Newsweek*, October 11, 1993, p. 42.

10. Bill Gates, Speech, WinHEC '97, San Francisco, California, April 8, 1997.

11. Peter Lewis, "Changing Channels," *PC World*, November 1997, p. 182.

12. Doug Abrams, "Gates Shares Dreams, Fears for Computers," *The Washington Times*, December 4, 1995, p. 10.

13. "Interview: Gordon Moore, Intel," *PC Magazine*, March 25, 1997.

14. Bill Gates, Speech, Microsoft Corporation Empowerment 2001, Seattle, Washington, February 9, 1998.

15. "Interview with Bill Gates, Microsoft," *PC Magazine*, March 25, 1997, p. 230.

16. Bill Gates, "When Will We See the Paperless Society," New York Times Syndicate, November 19, 1997.

17. Ibid.

18. Bill Gates, Column, New York Times Syndicate, January 29, 1997.

19. Ibid.

20. William Plummer, "Paul Allen," *People*, June 19, 1995, p. 105.

21. Robin Raskin, "What Next?" *Family PC*, March 1977.

22. Bill Gates, Speech, Office '97 Launch, New York, January 16, 1997.

23. Randall E. Stross, "Mr. Gates Builds His Brain Trust," *Fortune*, December 8, 1997.

24. Bill Gates, "Ask Bill," New York Times Syndicate, July 4, 1995.

25. "On the Future of Operating Systems," *PC World*, January 1998.

26. "Technology Titans Sound Off on the Digital Future," *U.S. News & World Report*, May 31, 1996.

27. Bill Gates, "Ask Bill," New York Times Syndicate, June 6, 1995.

28. Bill Gates, "Keeping Your Life From Becoming an Open Book," New York Times Special Features, November 5, 1996.

29. Bill Gates, "Localizing Reality in CD-ROM," The New York Times Syndicate, March 25, 1997.

30. Ibid.

31. Bill Gates, "Ask Bill," New York Times Syndicate, May 6, 1997.

Others Say

1. David Bank, "Microsoft Emphasizes Its Role as a Partner at Comdex," *The Wall Street Journal*, November 19, 1997, p. B4.

2. Steve Bass, "Today's Target: Microsoft," *PC World*, October, 1997, p. 320.

3. Robert X. Cringley, *Accidental Empires: How the Boys of Silicon Valley Make Their Millions, Battle Foreign Competition, and Still Can't Get a Date* (Reading, Mass: Addison-Wesley Publishing Co., 1992), pp. 115–116.

4. Ibid., p. 99.

5. Quotes, *Los Angeles Times*, December 31, 1997.

6. Julie Pitta, "Bill Gates and the Billophobes," *Forbes*, September 8, 1997, p. 188.

7. Ibid.

8. James Chposky and Ted Leonsis, *Blue Magic* (New York: Facts On File Publishing, 1988), p. 52.

9. Philip Elmer-DeWitt "Mine, All Mine," *Time*, June 5, 1996.

10. Stephen Manes and Paul Andrews, *Gates: How Microsoft's Mogul Reinvented an Industry—and Made Himself the Richest Man in America*, (New York: Doubleday, 1993) p. 405.

11. "Why Bill Gates Is Richer Than You," philg@mit.edu, April 1998.

12. Bradley Johnson, "Bill Gates' Vision of Microsoft in Every Home," *Advertising Age*, December 19, 1997.

13. Rich Karlgaard, "Silicon Valley's Politics of Envy," *The Wall Street Journal*, October 20, 1997, p. A20.

14. Intel press release, Business Wire, November 14, 1997.
15. Elmer-DeWitt "Mine, All Mine."
16. Bob Lewis, "So What If It's Not Your Idea—Steal It and Make It Work For You," *InfoWorld*, June 24, 1996.
17. Paul Somerson, "Blame Game," *PC Computing*, February 1998.
18. Bradley Johnson, "Renaissance Man Gates: Smart, Rich and Entirely Fun," *Advertising Age*, November 21, 1996.
19. Andrew Kupfer, "Gates on Buffett," *Fortune*, February 5, 1995.
20. Bill Gates, "What I Learned from Warren Buffett," *Harvard Business Review*, January/February 1996. Copyright 1995, Microsoft Corp.
21. Janet Lowe, *Warren Buffett Speaks: Wit and Wisdom from the World's Greatest Investor* (New York: John Wiley & Sons, 1996), p. 55.
22. Bill Gates, Column, New York Times Syndicate, March 12, 1997.
23. "The Gates Operating System," *Time*, January 13, 1997.
24. Video presentation, Berkshire Hathaway Annual Meeting, May 6, 1996.
25. Bill Gates, Keynote speech at San Jose State University, San Jose, Calif., January 27, 1998.
26. Jonathan R. Laing, "Baby Bust Ahead," *Barron's*, December 8, 1997, p. 37.
27. Gates, "What I Learned from Warren Buffett."
28. Alan Deutschman, "Bill Gates' Next Challenge," *Fortune*, December 28, 1992.
29. Bill Gates, "Focus on Technology," *Newsweek*, November 27, 1995, p. 65.
30. "They Said It," *Sports Illustrated*, June 16, 1997.

Living at the Pinnacle

1. Randall E. Stross, "Bill Gates: Richest American Ever," *Fortune*, August 4, 1997, p. 38.
2. Bills @ www:\\ nucalf.physics.fus.edu
3. Elise O'Shaughnessy, "The New Establishment," *Vanity Fair*, October 1994, p. 209.
4. Robert McMorris, "My Neighbor, Pal, Warren Buffett," *Omaha World Herald*, October 10, 1993.
5. "William Henry Gates III," *Forbes*, October 17, 1994, p. 103.
6. Bill Gates, Column, New York Times Syndicate, October 22, 1996.
7. Mortimer Zuckerman, "Zinging in the New Year," *U.S. News & World Report*, January 8, 1996, p. 64.
8. Newsbytes, on-line magazine, May 5, 1988.
9. Rodney Ho, "Autograph Hunter Solicits CEOs; Not All Send Warmest Regards," *The Wall Street Journal*, February 11, 1998.
10. The Smoking Gun Web Site, Archive.
11. *United States of America* v. *Adam Quinn Pletcher*, United States District Court Western District of Washington at Seattle, May 9, 1997.
12. Ibid.
13. Tim Klass, "Man Convicted of Threat to Gates," *Seattle Times*, March 25, 1998.

14. Mark Stevens, "Revenge of the Nerd," *M Inc.*, December 1990, p. 86.

15. G. Zachary Pascal, *Show Stopper! The Breakneck Race to Create Windows NT and the Next Generation at Microsoft* (New York: The Free Press, 1994), pp. 231–232.

16. Brian O'Reilly, "A Quartet of High-Tech Pioneers," *Fortune*, October 12, 1987.

17. Letter to Brent Wilde, Chief Appraiser, King's County Assessor's Office, Seattle, Washington, from Robert Chamberlain, Associate, Bruce C. Allen & Associates, Inc., July 24, 1995.

18. Gary McWilliams, "Michael Dell's Estate of Shock," *Business Week*, October 27, 1997.

19. Nancy Shute, "Houses Built to Move the Spirit—and Save Trees," *Smithsonian*, June 1996, p. 147.

20. Aaron Betsky, "The Cutler Edge," *Metropolitan Home*, May/June, 1996, p. 87.

21. Shute, "Houses Built to Move the Spirit."

22. Ibid.

23. Bill Gates, e-mail interview with author, April 30, 1998.

24. Sarah Medford, "Decorators at the Gates," *Town and Country Monthly*, July 1994, p. 13.

25. Richard Folkers, "Xanadu 2.0," *U.S. News & World Report*, December 1, 1997, p. 87.

26. Nancy Weil, "Gates to Critics: Sticks and Stones . . . " *Computerworld*, February 2, 1998.

27. Bill Gates with Nathan Myhrvold and Bill Rinearson, *The Road Ahead* (New York: Penguin Books, 1995), p. 248.

28. Margaret Talbot, "Seattle Diarist: Gates Heaven," *The New Republic*, October 20, 1997.

29. "Gates' Neighbors Not Awestruck," Associated Press, Medina, Washington, January 28, 1998.

30. Ibid.

31. John Cunningham, Driveways of the Rich & Famous, www.driveways.com.

32. "Of Bytes and Bites," *The New Yorker*, December 4, 1995, p. 38.

33. Ibid.

34. Richard Folkers, "Xanadu 2.0," *U.S. News & World Report*, December 1, 1997, p. 87.

35. Widely circulated on the Internet, original source uncertain.

36. "Money and Markets," *Fortune*, July 21, 1986, p. 24.

37. James Wallace and Jim Erickson, *Hard Drive* (New York: John Wiley & Sons, 1992), p. 240.

38. Distilled from messages on the Open Discussion Forum, February 9, 1998.

39. Stewart Deck, "Where Do You Want to Go Today? How About 20/20?" *Computerworld*, January 30, 1998.

40. Brian O'Reilly, "A Quartet of High-Tech Pioneers," *Fortune*, October 12, 1987, p. 149.

41. The Associated Press, "He's No Cheapskate: Bill Gates Gives Colleges $1.2 Million in Computers," *Newsday*, June 3, 1997, p. A 37.

42. Kate Bohner Lewis, "Forbes Informer," *Forbes*, January 22, 1996, p. 18.

43. "Bill Gates Donates Money to School," Associated Press, November 26, 1997.

44. "Gates Foundation to Invest $400 Million in Libraries," *American Libraries*, August, 1997, p. 14.

45. Bill Gates, "Closing the Information Gap," New York Times Syndicate, May 21, 1996.

46. Evan St. Lifer, "Gates Speaks to Librarians," *Library Journal*, July 1997, p. 44.

47. The Associated Press, "He's No Cheapskate."

48. Bill Gates, "Ask Bill," New York Times Syndicate, August 1, 1995.

49. Bill Gates, "Ask Bill," New York Times Syndicate, October 22, 1996.

50. Iibid.

51. John Seabrook, "Gates at the Temple," *The New Yorker*, December 11, 1995, p. 78.

52. Hugues Henry, "Let's Pie! Let's Pie! Nincompoop Guys!" *The Netley News*, February 9, 1998.

53. Ibid.

54. George Vernadakis, "Monica Speaks: A Pie Under the Lamp," *Inter-@ctive Week*, February 17, 1998.

Little Time for Love

1. "Money & Markets," *Fortune*, July 21, 1986, p. 24.

2. "Computer Mating," *People*, April 12, 1993, p. 71.

3. "Now Hear This," *Fortune*, May 17, 1993.

4. Daniel Ichbiah and Susan L. Knepper, *The Making of Microsoft* (Rocklin, Calif.: Prima Publishing, 1991), p. 221.

5. David Rensin, "The Bill Gates Interview," *Playboy*, December 8, 1994.

6. Janet Lowe, *Warren Buffett Speaks* (New York: John Wiley & Sons, 1997), p. 36.

7. John Seabrook, "E-Mail from Bill," *The New Yorker*, January 10, 1994, p. 48.

8. Warren Buffett, memo to Janet Lowe, July 21, 1998.

9. David Ellis, "Love Bytes," *People*, January 17, 1994, p. 42.

10. Chuck Taylor, "Gates, Journalist Settle Suit Over Wedding Arrest," *The Seattle Times*, April 13, 1995, p. B3.

11. Lynn Povich, "On Line with Bill Gates," *Working Woman*, January 1996, p. 41.

12. Brent Schlender, "Bill and Paul Talk," *Fortune*, October 2, 1998, p. 69.

13. O. Casey Corr, "Melinda French Gates: A Microsoft Mystery," *The Seattle Times*, June 4, 1995, p. C1.

14. Ibid.

15. Bill Gates Diary, *Slate*, March 2, 1998.

16. Bill Gates, e-mail interview with author, April 30, 1998.

17. "Computer Mating."

18. Bill Gates, e-mail interview with author, April 30, 1998.

19 Bill Gates, Speech, Detroit Economics Club, Detroit, Michigan, April 28, 1997.

20. Bill Gates, Speech, Comdex '97, Las Vegas, Nevada, November 16, 1997.

21. Bill Gates, Keynote speech, San Jose State University, San Jose, California, January 27, 1998.

22. "Verbatim," *Time*, May 13, 1996, p. 33.

The New Computer Culture

1. Bill Gates, "I Wish I Were a Kid Again," www.microsoft.com, February 28, 1995.

2. Susan Lammers, *Programmers at Work* (Redmond, Wash.: Microsoft Press, 1986), p. 89.

3. Bill Gates, Column, New York Times Syndicate, July 2, 1996.

4. Robin Raskin, "A Chat with Bill Gates," *Family PC*, March 1977.

5. "Business Times Web Event," *The Business Times* (Johannesburg, South Africa), March 6, 1997.

6. Bill Gates, Speech, Newspaper Association of America, Chicago, Illinois, April 29, 1997.

7. Bill Gates, Speech sponsored by the City of Chicago and the Chicago Public Library, March 19, 1996.

8. Bill Gates, "Ask Bill," New York Times Syndicate, September 26, 1995.

9. Bill Gates, "Support Freedom of Speech on the Internet," www.microsoft.com, 1997.

10. "The Microsoft Sell for Kids," *MacLeans*, August 5, 1996, p. 8.

11. Bill Gates, Speech, Learn Education Conference, Seattle, Washington, June 30, 1997.

12. Lance Morrow, "Hooray for Bill Gates . . . I Guess," *Time*, January 13, 1997, p. 84.

13. Bill Gates, "Ask Bill," New York Times Syndicate, February 15, 1995.

14. Brent Schlender, "What Does Bill Gates Want," *Fortune*, January 16, 1995, p. 40.

15. Bill Gates, "Technology," *The Costco Connection*, January 1998.

16. Bill Gates, "Ask Bill," New York Times Syndicate, April 10, 1996.

17. Bill Gates, "Ask Bill," New York Times Syndicate, November 22, 1995.

18. Carol J. Williams, "In the Kremlin, a Computer Czar," *Los Angeles Times*, October 11, 1997.

19. Ibid.

20. "Market Facts: Internet Emerges as Significant Medium for Consumers' News Usage," M2 Communications Ltd., www.tryloncommunications.com.

21. Bill Gates, "Banking on a Web Lifestyle," New York Times Special Features, July 15, 1997.

22. Bill Gates, Speech, National Governors' Association, Las Vegas, Nevada, July 30, 1997.

23. Bill Gates, Speech, Harvard Conference on Internet Society, Boston, Massachusetts, May 29, 1996.

24. Bill Gates, "Looking Back at Comdex," New York Times Special Features, December 3, 1996.

25. "Gates: From OS to Internet," *PC Week Online*, May 30, 1996.

26. John Seabrook, "E-Mail from Bill," *The New Yorker*, January 10, 1994, p. 55.

27. Bill Gates, Speech, Fall Comdex, Las Vegas, Nevada, November 19, 1996.

28. Bill Gates, Speech, Small Business Server Crossings, Redmond, Washington, October 28, 1997.

29. Bill Gates, Speech, Comdex '97, Las Vegas, Nevada, November 16, 1997.

30. Bill Gates, Speech, Newspaper Association of America, Chicago,.

31. Bill Gates, "Technology," p. 23.

32. Bill Gates, Speech, Microsoft Site Builder Conference, Seattle, Washington, October 30, 1996.

33. Bill Gates, Speech, Professional Developers Conference, San Francisco, California, March 13, 1996.

34. Roy Furchgott, "Guess the Check Is in the E-mail," *Business Week*, February 19, 1998.

35. "Fake Bill Gates Talks Windows 95 on AOL," Newsbytes News Network, August 22, 1995.

36. Bill Gates, "Focus on Technology," *Newsweek*, November 27, 1995, p. 68.

37. Daniel Burstein and David Kline, *Road Warriors: Dreams and Nightmares Along the Information Highway* (New York: Dutton, 1995), p. 210.

38. John Wilke and David Bank, "Gates Answers to Criticism of Microsoft," *The Wall Street Journal*, March 3, 1998.

39. Bill Gates, e-mail interview with author, April 30, 1998.

40. "In Their Own Words," *The Wall Street Journal*, March 4, 1998, p. B1.

41. Bill Gates, Speech, Massachusetts Institute of Technology Distinguished Lecture Series, Boston, Massachusetts, May 30, 1996.

42. Bill Gates, e-mail interview with author, April 30, 1998.

43. Bill Gates, "Networks or Nations?" *New Perspectives Quarterly*, Spring, 1995, p. 51.

44. "The Secret Diary of Bill Gates," www.tiac.net/users/BillG40/BillGates2.htm

45. Richard M. Smith, "Bill's Excellent Future," *Newsweek*, October 11, 1993, p. 42.

46. Bill Gates, with Nathan Myhrvold and Peter Rinearson, *The Road Ahead* (New York: Penguin Books, 1955), p. 308.

47. Nathan Gardees, "A Democratic Media," *New Perspectives Quarterly*, Spring 1995, p. 50.

48. Yael Li-Ron, "Gates: Hated and Admired," *PC World*, January 16, 1998.

49. Rich Karlgaard, "On the Road with Bill Gates," *Forbes ASAP*, February 28, 1994.

50. Michael Dertouzos, "Friction-free Capitalism and Electronic Bulldozers," *New Perspectives Quarterly*, March 22, 1997, p. 15.

51. Bill Gates, Speech, Detroit Economic Club, Detroit, Michigan, April 29, 1997.

52. "Gates Opens Up for Questions," *Computerworld*, The Internet, October 6, 1997.

53. Ibid.

54. Bill Gates, "Ask Bill," New York Times Syndicate, March 13, 1996.

55. Bill Gates, "Technology, Education and Income," New York Times Special Features, June 19, 1997.

56. Bill Gates, Speech, Microsoft/NEC Videoconference, Redmond, Washington, and Tokyo, Japan, August 26, 1997.

57. Laurie Kretchmar, "Interview with Bill Gates," *Working Woman*, April, 1994, p. 62.

58. Jeff James, "Letters," *Time*, June 26, 1995, p. 4.

Gates on Life

1. Bill Gates, Column, New York Times Syndicate, February 12, 1997.

2. Brent Schlender, "What Does Bill Gates Really Want," *Fortune*, January 16, 1995, p. 35.

3. Bill Gates, Column, New York Times Syndicate, March 13, 1996.

4. Bill Gates, Column, New York Times Syndicate, July 1, 1997.

5. *Larry King Live*, CNN, August 21, 1995.

6. Ibid.

7. Bill Gates, "Ask Bill," New York Times Syndicate, January 17, 1995.

8. Ibid.

9. Lee Rosenbaum, "Leonardo in D-drive," *Art in America*, December 1996, p. 25.

10. Bill Gates, "Technology," *The Costco Connection*, January 1998.

11. Bill Gates, "Ask Bill," New York Times Syndicate, May 9, 1995.

12. Bill Gates, "Ask Bill," New York Times Syndicate, December 17, 1996.

13. John Mariotti, "Where Have All the Heroes Gone?" *Industry Week*, January 8, 1996, p. 25.

14. "Letters," *Time*, February 10, 1997, p. 10.

15. "Quotes," *Los Angeles Times*, December 31, 1997.

16. "In Search of the Real Bill Gates," *Time*, January 13, 1997.

17. Rich Karlgaard, "On the Road with Bill Gates," *Forbes ASAP*, February 28, 1994.

18. Frank Rich, "Love that Bill," *The New York Times*, March 7, 1998, p. A13.

The Bottom Line

1. Randall E. Stross, *The Microsoft Way: The Real Story of How the Company Outsmarts Its Competition* (Reading, Mass.: Addison-Wesley, 1996) p. 5.

2. Bill Gates, "Watching His Windows," *Forbes ASAP*, December 1, 1997, p. 142.

3. Alan Duetschman, "Bill Gates' Next Challenge," *Fortune*, December 28, 1992.

4. Bill Gates, "Ask Bill," New York Times Syndicate, September 23, 1997.

5. Philip Elmer-DeWitt and David S. Jackson, "Hard Drive," *Time*, June 5, 1995.

6. Charles Cooper, "Gates: Staying Put Until My 50s," *PCWeek Online*, April 4, 1997.

7. Bill Gates, Speech, Kellogg Technology Series, Evanston, Illinois, April 29, 1997.

8. Bill Gates, e-mail interview with author, April 30, 1998.

9. Steven Levy, "Bill's New Vision," *Newsweek*, November 27, 1995, p. 56.

10. Bill Gates, Column, New York Times Syndicate, September 23, 1997.

11. Bill Gates, Column, New York Times Syndicate, July 1, 1997.

12. Bill Gates, "Biotechnology, Like Software, Will Change the World," New York Times Syndicate, June 19, 1996.

13. Karlgaard, "On the Road with Bill Gates."

14. "The Gates Operating System," *Time*, January 13, 1998.

15. Bill Gates, "Ask Bill," New York Times Syndicate, December 17, 1997.

16. Levy, "Bill's New Vision."

Lightning Source UK Ltd.
Milton Keynes UK
21 December 2010

164745UK00001B/1/A